Judaism, Addiction and Recovery
A Spiritual and Faith-based Approach

Richard L. Eisenberg
Rabbi, Certified Addictions Counselor

*For Lauren,
Without you, this may never have come to pass. Thanks so much for your guidance & inspiration.*

Rich

Mazo Publishers

Judaism, Addiction and Recovery:
A Spiritual and Faith-based Approach

ISBN 978-1-946124-57-9

Copyright © 2019 by Richard L. Eisenberg
Email: beyondthe12steps120@gmail.com

Published by:

Mazo Publishers
P.O. Box 10474 ~ Jacksonville, FL 32247 USA

Website: www.mazopublishers.com
Bookstore: www.mazopub.com

Front cover background image by
Annie Spratt | unsplash.com

54321
All rights reserved.
No part of this publication may be translated, reproduced, stored in a retrieval system, or transmitted in any form or by any means, electronic, mechanical, photocopying, recording or otherwise, without prior permission in writing from the publisher.

– For Judy –
My wife, best friend and fellow traveler on life's journey

CONTENTS

About the Author   6
Acknowledgments   7
Introduction   10
Prologue   16

Part One
THE SPIRITUAL FOG OF ADDICTION ~ 23

1. "Jews Don't Use" – Myth upon Myth   24
2. In the Closet   27
3. Eyes Wide Shut   32
4. Medical vs. Moral   38
5. Not our Fault   46
6. Our Moral Institutions   53
7. Cultural and Religious Identity   60
8. The Spiritual Fog of Addiction   66
9. Moving Towards Change   75

Part Two
LIFTING THE FOG ~ 85

1. The "Miracle" of Recovery   86
2. From Preparation to Action   90
3. Getting out of the Way   96
4. Intervention, Treatment and Self-Help   103
5. The Wide Wide World of Treatment   108
6. The View from the Grandstand   115
7. Addiction, Compassion and Forgiveness   122
8. Experiencing Treatment   127
9. Termination and Transition   136

Part Three
RECOVERY AND RETURN ~ 143

1. Into the Wilderness   144
2. Reentering the Camp   148
3. Paying it Forward   153
4. PAWS   159

Epilogue   166

About the Author

Rabbi Richard L. Eisenberg was born in Bridgeport, CT, received a BA in Anthropology from Duke University, MA in Religious Studies from Smith College, Rabbinical Ordination from the Jewish Theological Seminary and a Certificate in Drug and Alcohol Recovery Counseling from Gateway Community College.

Over a span of 35 years, he served as a congregational rabbi in Columbus, GA, Wayne, NJ, Woodbridge, CT and Torrington, CT. He is a certified addictions counselor and worked as a rehabilitation counselor for almost a decade at the APT Foundation, a treatment center in New Haven, CT. He has written for Tablet Magazine and the Forward and is currently working on a book that analyzes modern-day addictions and attachments from a spiritual perspective.

Rabbi Eisenberg lives with his wife Judy in Hamden, CT.

Acknowledgments

I extend deepest gratitude and appreciation to...

My teachers at the Jewish Theological Seminary who helped me understand how Jewish texts and traditions continue to resonate in the modern world; colleagues and friends in the rabbinate; former congregants who were receptive to my teaching, support and pastoral care and who offered their support in turn; Peggy Whelan, who served as my clinical supervisor and was instrumental in training me to become an addictions counselor; Lauren Doninger and Cher Shannon: Dr. Doninger who, in her capacity as Director of Gateway Community College's Drug and Alcohol Recovery Counselor program (DARC), helped guide my transition from a full-time rabbinic career into the counseling field; Cher Shannon, who took over the Director position during my time at Gateway and presided over my yearlong internship seminar; Jane Tendler, who, as Human Resources Director of the APT Foundation, strongly encouraged me to do my internship there and later hired me as a counselor; my former colleagues and patients at the APT Foundation; Rabbi Carl Astor and the aforementioned Peggy Whelan for carefully reading my manuscript and offering thoughtful critiques; literary agent Jonathan Agin for his useful suggestions and advice; my publisher Chaim Mazo who was willing to accept this book for publication, a book dealing with a subject that many would choose to avoid.

I also thank my personal friends, both inside and outside my professional life and whose names are too numerous to mention here, who have stuck with me throughout the years; my mother Ellie who, at age 91, remains one of the sweetest, kindest people on God's earth and an exceptionally devoted mother; her twin brother Dick Davis who has always been like a father to me and has been one of my role models for his tireless energy and his ability to set and achieve high goals for himself; my father Marshall (z"l) for teaching me civility and the ability to relate to almost anyone and who would never tolerate hearing anyone say a negative word about me; my sister Sue (z"l) for her unconditional love, her readiness to switch careers and try new things and her courage as she lived with cancer for 3½ years before moving onto the hereafter; my children Sam and Rebecca and her husband Chris for their patience with me and their ability to forgive

Acknowledgments

and overlook my mistakes and failures as a parent; and finally, my wife and life partner Judy: no words can begin to express how much you mean to me and the extent of your unflinching support through thick and thin. I love you more now than ever.

One further note: For Biblical quotations I referred to the Jewish Publication Society translation of the Tanakh (Holy Scriptures).

מִן הַמֵּצַר קָרָאתִי יָּהּ עָנָנִי בַמֶּרְחָב יָהּ:

In my distress I called on the Lord;
The Lord answered me and brought me relief.

(Psalm 118:5)

Help me if you can, I'm feeling down –
And I do appreciate you being 'round.
Help me get my feet back on the ground –
Won't you please, please help me?

John Lennon, Paul McCartney (from "Help" by the Beatles)

Introduction

We Jews have a lot to learn about addiction. It is striking that the people who produced Freud, Einstein, Salk and so many other pioneers in medicine and science can be so backward regarding addiction. We say we accept the Disease Model of addiction yet we stigmatize and isolate those who suffer as well as their families. We hold on to the false notion that other cultures, ethnicities and socio-economic groups produce more addicts than we do. We establish treatment centers that fail to provide the necessary medication for opioid dependent patients, wrongly claiming that they cannot be "clean" while taking methadone, buprenorphine or naltrexone. We provide community resources and support for those same treatment centers that provide pseudo-12 Step models in the guise of real treatment. At the same time, our synagogues and community centers shy away from opening their doors to 12 Step meetings such as Alcoholics Anonymous (AA), Narcotics Anonymous (NA) or Al-Anon (for family and friends of addicted people). We use Hebrew and religious concepts like *Teshuvah* (Return, Repentance) to broadly describe recovery but ignore how these concepts can wrongly imply that the recovering addict is a sinner who is repenting. We look down on people with addiction, especially when they are unable to sustain jobs or careers. We judge their families for their inability to prevent or solve their chemical dependence.

Addiction is an offender that knows no cultural and religious bounds. The Jewish culture is no exception. Few studies have thoroughly investigated the phenomenon of addiction among Jews; to my knowledge, few Jewish authors have tried to present a fair, open-minded approach to the problem of Jews and addiction.

From what I have seen, an underlying assumption among Jewish pundits on addiction has, for decades, stalled the Jewish community's ability to discuss addiction in ways that can benefit the most people: the assumption that recovery ought to go hand in hand with 12 Step programs and the need to demonstrate the compatibility between Judaism and the 12 Steps. The latter has already been demonstrated effectively in worthy books by rabbis over the past thirty years. There's no need to keep reissuing the same themes under different packages. The former may have made some sense years ago but is now becoming

Introduction

less valid. Much as I admire the 12 Steps and many aspects of 12 Step programs, they do not work for everyone. To imagine otherwise is to delude oneself and others. This can be dangerous, especially in light of the current opioid epidemic. When it comes to treatment and recovery, no one size fits all.

What qualifies me to go out on a limb and say all this? Where do I get the *chutzpah* to critique Jewish approaches to addiction? Actually, my perspective offers little that is new or innovative. It is based on years of work in congregations and an outpatient clinic serving people with substance use disorders. My approach is based upon medical and Harm Reduction models[1], all evidence-based and backed by science and research. Through direct experience as a treatment provider, I have come to believe that the goal of reducing harm, supporting patients when their goal is to cut down on drug or alcohol use even when they're not ready to stop completely, is both valid and necessary.

It took me a long time to reach these conclusions. I served as a synagogue rabbi for 35 years. Rarely did I encounter congregants or their families who were affected by substance use disorders. I know they were out there but they were in hiding. My eyes were opened when I encountered addiction in my own family. I felt like I was being kicked in the gut, every day, constantly. I turned to a self-help program for families of alcoholics, where I found considerable support and guidance. At the same time, I heard many stories told by Alcoholics Anonymous members describing the nightmarish process that landed them into the program. Time and time again I heard it said that total abstinence is the only path in recovery. AA veterans of twenty, thirty years and more spoke about how, even with all those years of sobriety behind them, they were just one step away from that one drink that could lead them back into full blown alcoholism. Hearing this, I

---

1 According to the Harm Reduction Coalition (www.harmreduction.org), Harm Reduction is "a set of practical strategies aimed at reducing the negative consequences of drug use," and is "a movement of social justice built on a belief in, and respect for, the rights of people who use drugs." The Harm Reduction model accepts that illicit drug use is part of contemporary life and tries to minimize its effect by recognizing that drug use is a complex continuum of behaviors; some ways of using are safer than others, and reduction in use may be a more realistic immediate goal for some people than total abstinence. Harm Reduction *does not* minimize or ignore the dangers of illicit use.

would be reminded of God's words to Cain after showing favoritism to Abel: "Why are you distressed, and why is your face fallen? Surely, if you do right, there is uplift. But if you do not do right, sin couches at the door; Its urge is toward you, yet you can be its master," (Genesis 4:6-7). Even for the alcoholic in long-term sobriety, that next drink couches at the door, tempting relapse, inviting disaster. But here's the big difference: God reminded Cain of his ability to exercise control over sin; the alcoholic in AA must admit powerlessness over alcohol, realizing his total inability to control his drinking. There's no such thing as only one drink. One turns into two, then five, then ten or more. The pattern becomes inexorable.

I came to believe that this was what it must be like for every person with alcoholism or drug addiction. Recovery meant total abstinence. But my eyes were opened when I began to take classes in a drug and alcohol recovery counseling program at Gateway Community College in New Haven. The teachers would tell us about Harm Reduction, an approach that defied earlier ways of understanding the nature of recovery. The Harm Reduction Model also encompassed several aspects of social and governmental policy (like needle exchanges and methadone programs), but I was especially intrigued – and challenged – by the notion that reducing one's drinking and drug use could actually be a recovery path. I still held on to the AA total abstinence idea because I was convinced by the stories and testimonies I had heard from AA members. So I questioned my teachers, did some reading, talked to some people in recovery who were not members of a 12 Step program. My thinking shifted as I opened my mind to the possibility, and reality, of people making honest and positive attempts to recover without being ready to completely give up their drug of choice.

Then I jumped into the deep waters of counseling at an outpatient clinic. As I began earning the hours necessary for certification as an addictions counselor, I served as an intern and was subsequently hired to provide individual and group counseling. I felt the same kind of trepidation I felt 25 years earlier when, as a new rabbi, I had to conduct my first funeral and wedding. Now I was working with a population consisting mostly of disenfranchised individuals from the greater New Haven area. I encountered clients who were fresh out of prison or trying to avoid it, mothers and fathers who were on the radar of Department of Children and Families trying to either keep parental custody or regain it, people who had histories of severe trauma who self-medicated and were seeking help, the mentally ill with co-occurring disorders who needed support. I had my successes and my failures, but I reached some clear conclusions over the course of my 10 years working at the clinic. First: treatment works, especially when it is delivered in a person-centered, compassionate and intelligent manner. Second: my patients ran the gamut from those deeply committed to recovery to those who were not yet ready. Even the latter had reason to seek treatment and chose to stay, and many of them possessed immense potential for growth and healing. Third: many of my patients were not yet ready to stop using their drug of choice or had already stopped but were struggling with another drug. But as they continued to cut down on their use, they showed impressive signs of progress in treatment. They may still have been doing some drinking or psychoactive drug using but they were doing it less and were noticing an improvement in their daily functioning and the reparation of social and familial relationships. Thus, my clinical experience taught me the important lesson that people can heal – mentally, emotionally, physically and spiritually – while reducing drug or alcohol intake. Recovery is not to be confined only to those who have achieved total abstinence.

The purpose of this book is to provide a newer perspective on addiction for Jews struggling with addiction and for their families, friends and supporters. It is an answer to those who talk about addiction as a disease while eschewing medically effective medication assisted treatments like methadone and buprenorphine. I hope to demonstrate the benefits of treatment in general and certain treatment modalities in particular. I will also mention some caveats about treatments that may not be as effective or helpful as they claim.

This volume is meant to be a work of outreach to all members of the Jewish community regardless of religious affiliations. It is also intended for the more secular-minded among us. Though I will be speaking at length about spirituality, this is not intended to be confused with religion. Surely, the two concepts can frequently overlap in a person, but it is possible (and common) to find those who have one without the other. Although the Prologue will attempt to deliver lessons from biblical and rabbinic teachings, this will be presented not as a religious commentary but rather as a brief historical overview of Judaism's views on intoxicants.

Part One will discuss what I call the spiritual fog of addiction from an experiential point of view. Though my perspective is fully grounded in the findings of science and research, my focus will be to share what I have learned, observed and taught throughout my career both as a rabbi and addictions counselor. Volumes and countless articles have been written by experts trying to determine the root causes of addiction. Though I believe the etiology of addiction is primarily biological, psychological, social and spiritual, it is not my intention to delve at length into the reasons people develop addictions. Instead, I will address myths about addiction in the Jewish community, issues of stigma and shame, the Moral versus Medical model of addiction, the plight of the affected individual and his family, the loneliness of isolation, what makes Jewish culture unique in the way it responds to addiction, how the erosion of Jewish identity can pave the way for higher risks of addiction.

Part Two will outline some considerations that emerge as the spiritual fog of addiction begins to lift once the person enters treatment and early recovery. I will explain different treatment modalities and options. I will show how 12 Step programs are NOT treatment; though 12 Step Principles can be utilized in treatment the programs themselves qualify as self-help and peer support. They are not meant to be clinical. Moreover, treatment centers that require attendance at AA or NA may be doing a disservice to their residents, especially those who are resistant to 12 Step principles and prefer other approaches. I will also share my concern about the way many adherents of 12 Step programs view their recovery path as the only valid one.

Part Two will also include a discussion of Jewish terms and concepts that are relevant to persons suffering from addiction as well as their families. Some concepts perpetuate the stigma and shame of addiction, others open the door for more understanding and compassion. I will also look at the challenges of re-entry into family and community and the roles of family members, friends, synagogues and other communal institutions in the addicted person's return.

The new life in sustained, long-term recovery will be the subject of Part Three. As the recovering person solidifies connections and relationships with family and community, some challenges and irritants do not automatically disappear. Fears of relapse can linger, suspicion among family members and friends can persist. Post Acute Withdrawal Syndrome (PAWS) can continue for up to a few years after the date of last use. (More will be said about PAWS in Section Three.) Memories and flashbacks can pop up at any time in the mind of the formerly addicted person and his family, causing distress and elevated

Introduction

anxiety. Members of the community tend to hold on to stigmatizing and shaming attitudes. The Jewish community is now charged with the responsibility to provide a warm, welcoming and non-judgmental presence for all those affected by the addiction.

This book is not meant to be a comprehensive look at addiction issues in the Jewish community, nor does it address addictions outside of chemical dependence such as pathological gambling, sex and eating disorders.[2] Instead, it is designed to be the start of what I hope will be a new direction in the ways we Jews talk and think about addiction. I acknowledge that many of you are reading these pages because you or someone you know is suffering from the disease of addiction. Others may be reading this more out of the desire to learn about an epidemic that active threatens our society. Either way, please know that your interest and openness to such a difficultly subject can only bear positive results.

One further note: This volume is written from a Jewish perspective, however I believe it can benefit all who are willing to see spiritual and/or faith-based dimensions in the phenomena of addiction and recovery. Thus, I commend this book to anyone, Jewish or non-Jewish, who is seeking an articulation of the right questions as well as some possible solutions to one of the most challenging and threatening crises of our time.

---

2   Treatment of these addictions is outside my field of expertise, though many of the insights and suggestions contained in this volume could be easily applied to addictive disorders other than chemical dependence.

Prologue

Biblical and Rabbinic attitudes concerning wine depend on context. Wine is considered positive when used for sacramental or recreational purposes in moderation. The negative references focus on wine's intoxicating effects, especially loss of judgment. The sacramental elements include the use of wine for Kiddush on Shabbat and festivals and for sacrificial libations during Biblical times until the destruction of the Second Temple in 70 CE. Allusions to the recreational uses of wine include such verses as "wine that cheers the hearts of men" (Psalm 104:15) and several passages in Song of Songs. Taken together, all these references view wine as part of God's creation and as a way of enhancing life's experiences.

However, the negative treatment of wine in other contexts is more vivid and powerful. Consider the two most conspicuous examples in Genesis, both involving alcohol consumption to the point of blacking out: The first, in Genesis chapter 9 describes Noah's drunkenness and nakedness, behaviors that were mocked by his son Ham; the second (Genesis 19) involved Lot's daughters' successful scheme to ply their father with wine after the destruction of Sodom. Believing that with Sodom's annihilation God had indeed wiped out the entire world, the daughters felt compelled to carry on the human race by tricking Lot into having sex with them while in a drunken state.

Two other references to wine consumption, both more indirect than the last two, can be found in the Torah. In Genesis 27 Rebecca overhears Isaac's plan to bless Esau over a plate of delicious venison stew that Esau would prepare after going out to hunt game. Because Jacob is her favorite, she immediately hatches a ruse to fool Isaac by disguising Jacob as Esau and having him bring Isaac an equally delicious helping of lamb stew. As Jacob draws near his father, Isaac immediately grows suspicious. Nevertheless, the scheme appears to be working. Yet Isaac still isn't sure. "He asked, 'Are you really my son Esau?' And when he said 'I am,' he said, 'Serve me and let me eat of my son's game that I may give you my innermost blessing.' So he served him and he ate, and he brought him wine and he drank (Genesis 27:24-25)." Apparently, Isaac may have imbibed enough wine to confuse his taste buds so that he imagined the lamb stew was really made from venison. And the wine may have intoxicated him

Prologue

enough to cloud his judgment, thereby guaranteeing the success of Rebecca's and Jacob's underhanded plan.

The second reference occurs in Leviticus chapter 10, the episode of Nadav and Avihu, two of Aaron's sons. The Torah relates a strange incident when the two sons bring an *aish zara,* "alien fire" (an unwarranted incense offering) that God "had not enjoined upon them (Leviticus 9:1)." God immediately responds by sending down a fire to incinerate them and cryptically explains the punishment by having Moses tell Aaron, "This is what the Lord meant when He said: 'Through those near to me I show myself holy, and gain glory before all the people (Leviticus 9:3)." What follows is a description of the removal of the sons' bodies and instructions to Aaron and the remaining sons not to mourn, whereas the rest of the people were to mourn. Then, all of a sudden, God addresses Aaron: "Drink no wine or other intoxicant, you or your sons, when you enter the Tent of Meeting, that you may not die… (Leviticus 10:9)." Since this warning almost immediately follows the deaths of Nadav and Avihu, it is plausible that they brought the "alien fire" while intoxicated and their excessive imbibing led to a lapse in judgment and a breach against the realm of the holy.[1] Alternatively, were the warning to be understood separately from the preceding episode, the meaning would still be similar: Wine can impair judgment and dull the senses, causing the priests to err during the performance of their sacrificial duties.

To sum up: Wine can be used for good or for ill. When used for ill, a few questions emerge. In addition to blackouts and lapses in judgment, do the Bible or rabbinic Sages have anything to say about the addictive qualities of wine? If so, would they have considered the addiction chronic or reversible? And if chronic, could the condition somehow be manageable?

Wine is mentioned many times in the Bible and rabbinic literature, s*hekhar* (another intoxicating beverage, possibly beer or a stronger form of wine) less so. Since I do not intend to provide a comprehensive study on the treatment of wine in ancient Jewish sources, I will comment on only two texts, one from Proverbs, the other from the Midrash.

The author of Proverbs was extremely wary of wine and its harmful effects. He must have observed enough people who drank excessively to include several warnings about wine in his book of

---

1 See Rashi's commentary on Leviticus 10:2 (Rashi was the great 11th century French commentator on the Holy Scriptures and Talmud).

moral teachings. In chapter 23, he first cautions that gluttony and alcoholism lead to impoverishment. Later in the chapter, he describes the damaging effects of excessive drinking in vivid terms:

> "Who cries 'Woe,' who 'Alas'! Who has quarrels, who complaints; who has wounds without cause; who has bleary eyes? Those whom wine keeps till the small hours, those who gather to drain the cups. Do not ogle that red wine as it lends its color to the cup, as it flows on smoothly; In the end it bites like a snake, it spits like a basilisk. Your eyes will see strange sights, your heart will speak distorted things. You will be like one lying in bed on high seas. Like one lying on top of the rigging. 'They struck me but I felt no hurt; they beat me but I was unaware; *as often as I wake I go after it again*' (Proverbs 23:29-35, italics mine)."

This is the Bible's most comprehensive statement against the excessive use of wine. It covers the physical and psychological effects. The writer refers to hallucinations and dementia, nausea, sleep disorder, blackout and oblivion. The medieval commentators Rashi and Ibn Ezra see a reference to self-medication and escape from pain in these verses. What is perhaps most remarkable is the last phrase, "as often as I wake I go after it again." The commentaries link this phrase with the first half of the verse to indicate the drinker's tendency to use wine to escape from or mask pain. Whether this is so, the last phrase clearly describes a condition of alcohol dependence, the compulsion to drink constantly, even upon waking, in order to avoid withdrawal symptoms.

We can conclude from this passage in Proverbs that the Bible not only recognized the harmful outcomes of excessive drinking but the addictive qualities of intoxicants. The writer's warning included a strong admonition: "Do not ogle that red wine...," that is, stay away from wine altogether if you are susceptible to its addictive properties. One might argue that the Biblical author was advocating a position of total abstinence. The only solution for a person who drinks too much is to avoid drinking altogether.

In the Rabbinic literature such as the Talmud and books of Midrash (mostly non-legal texts and commentaries), the Sages expanded upon the Biblical admonitions against excessive drinking. All the themes listed above are reinforced; the loss of judgment, distortion of the senses, impoverishment and inability to function properly. Some texts (e.g. Midrash Tanhuma Noah:18) describe the progression from moderate to heavy drinking and the accompanying effects: the moderate drinker feels "strong as a lion," when he imbibes too much he resembles a pig, when he becomes intoxicated he acts like a monkey, "he dances around, sings, talks obscenely, and knows not what he is doing."[2] Another source (Midrash Rabba on Numbers 10:8) suggests that a person loses a quarter of his intellect after drinking one cup of wine, half his intellect after two cups, after the third he becomes confused and speaks incoherently, after the fourth he is unable to speak. Therefore, the Sages recognized that while wine could have beneficial qualities they cautioned against immoderate use.

One particularly fascinating Rabbinic passage points to the complexity of alcoholism as a condition that affects both the addicted individual and his family. It is found in the Midrash Rabbah on Leviticus (Shemini 12:1):

> Rabbi Isaac ben Redifa said in the name of Rabbi Ammi: In the end he [the excessive drinker] sells his household articles, and drinks wine with the proceeds. Rabbi Aha said: There is a story of a man who kept on selling his household goods and drinking wine with the proceeds. Said his sons, 'Our father will leave nothing for us.' So they plied him with drink, and made him drunk, and took him out and placed him in a cemetery. Wine merchants passed the gate of the cemetery, and hearing that a seizure for public service [i.e. forced labor] was to take place in the province, they left their loads within the cemetery and went to witness the uproar in the province. The man, waking up from his sleep and seeing a [wine]skin bottle above his head, untied it and put it in his mouth. Three days later his sons said: 'Should we not go to see what father is doing?' They went and found him with the wine-skin in his mouth. They said: 'Even here your Creator has not forsaken you. Seeing that he has given you [wine], we do not know what we should do to you.' They made an arrangement amongst themselves that the sons should in turn provide him with drink, one son one day.[3]

---

2   Louis Ginzberg, The Legends of the Jews, (Philadelphia: The Jewish Publication Society of America, 1968), Volume 1, p.168.

3   Rev. J. Israelstam trans., Midrash Rabbah: Leviticus (London, New York: Soncino Press), p. 153.

Prologue

What is this midrash trying to say? Since it is found in the section containing Midrash commentaries on the Leviticus story of Nadav and Avihu, it is safe to assume that its starting point is the ill effects of too much wine consumption. In the case of Nadav and Avihu, the Midrash assumes a link between their brazen act of bringing an unwarranted incense offering and the supposition that they did so because they were intoxicated. In other words, too much wine impairs judgment. If you are a priest in a position of power and honor like Aaron's two sons, the results can be devastating.

By bringing in the story of the father who drinks away his property, the Midrash is adding several serious considerations to the problem of immoderate drinking. Nadav and Avihu may have liked their wine, maybe too much, and this led to their deaths. But there is no indication in the text that they drank *alcoholically*. Our father in the story clearly suffers from alcoholism. His condition causes him to sell his property to support his compulsion. So far, the Midrash adds nothing that we haven't seen in the other Biblical texts cited above.

What's new is the dimension of alcoholism's effects on the family, in this case the two sons. Plus, their solution at the story's conclusion is especially meaningful.

At first, the sons are at least partly motivated by self-interest ("Our father will leave nothing for us"). They are worried that they will lose their inheritance if he keeps drinking. They falsely believe that they can get him to stop drinking by scaring him to death, signified by getting him drunk and dropping him off in a cemetery! When they finally realize that no intervention on their part will cause him to find sobriety, they come up with a creative solution. They decide to take turns providing him with wine. No longer will he drink away his possessions. Now each son will help fund his addiction. They resign themselves to the conclusion that their father will continue to drink no matter what they do, and they come to accept the reality of his condition.

It may appear that the father hit his "bottom" once he awoke in the cemetery with the empty wine skin in his mouth. But unlike the bottom spoken of by AA members, this bottom doesn't lead him to sobriety. *Is it possible that it leads him to a moderation in his level of drinking?* Perhaps his sons, having admitted their powerlessness over getting him to stop, are now able to help him drink less excessively by rationing his wine intake on a daily basis.

Could this be an early form of medication assisted treatment and

Harm Reduction? Could it be that the father's daily intake of wine is now controlled and no longer will he drink to the point of blackout? No longer will he need to sell his property in order to support his addiction. His sons will now offer him sufficient amounts of wine to eliminate his cravings and any withdrawal symptoms. Perhaps he will drink enough to be comfortable and not too much to be disabled.

This remarkable midrash teaches lessons that resonate today. Some people with addiction problems can actually find ways to function and even get better without totally eliminating their drug of choice. Or they may find other medications that take away drug cravings and withdrawals and help them to recover. Their family members will support them best by coming alongside them *wherever they are* in their level of interaction with their drug of choice (with notable exceptions as discussed below) instead of swimming upstream and vainly trying to make them change. That is not to suggest that the family members should approve of their loved one's maladaptive behaviors. But by attaining a level of acceptance of the addiction and its nature, effected families and friends can re-channel energy that had previously been wasted into new ways of helping and supporting their addicted loved one.

Rabbi Aha in the Midrash seemed to have understood this. It is time that we do too. The spiritual fog of addiction prevents us – addicted individuals, their family and friends, and Jewish treatment providers – from seeing clearly that addiction and recovery are not simple matters. There is little here that is black and white. Thoughtful and open-minded responses are called for. Far too much is at stake to over-simplify what is so complex.

Part One

THE SPIRITUAL FOG OF ADDICTION

Chapter 1

"Jews Don't Use" – Myth upon Myth

I wrote this book as a wake-up call to the Jewish community, challenging us to stop pretending that chemical dependence is something that happens to other cultures and social groups. Especially in a time of crisis, with the opioid epidemic raging around us, lives hang in the balance. Either we will choose to pay attention or opt for apathy and indifference, with tragic consequences.

"Jews Don't Use" has been a commonly mentioned notion within American Jewry for decades. It became a popular myth when enough Jews really started to believe that problem drinking and drugging were scarce among Jews. The myth assumed prejudicial proportions when it took aim at substance abuse among gentiles; "A shikker is a goy, (a drunk must be gentile)," with its insulting messages and innuendos, implied that Jewish people don't suffer from alcoholism or drug addiction. Instead, it's a gentile problem. It's the Irish who drink, or the Italians. It's the African Americans who shoot heroin and smoke crack. But Jews? God Forbid! Couldn't possibly be.

While I was growing up in the 50s and 60s, my parents would sometimes talk about three of my uncles and their proclivity for gambling. No one said they were gambling addicts, but my uncles liked to play the horses and trade on margins in the stock market. One of my uncles also was involved in bootlegging in the 1920s and helped smuggle whiskey from Canada. According to family legend, he played poker with Dutch Schultz at the Stratford Hotel in Bridgeport, CT. This uncle was one of my favorites because he was fun to be with. I loved spending time with him, but he rarely talked about his past exploits.

During the first half of the 20th century gambling became a common problem among Jews. So, perhaps, did alcoholism. But these addictive behaviors weren't talked about very much. Addiction to narcotics would have been even less recognized. A Jewish drug addict? A *shonda*! Unimaginable! A Jew using heroin? Impossible! Except for the hidden few whom nobody spoke of, shunned by their families and community, existing underground, eventually dying penniless and alone.

I remember seeing Frank Sinatra's stirring performance in "The Man with the Golden Arm" when I was a child and thinking, "This would never happen to a Jew, a Jew shooting up dope, never." I was too young to understand that the notion of Jewish immunity to addictions like heroin, alcohol or cocaine is an illusion.

Other than an inconclusive survey conducted by JACS (Jewish Alcoholics, Chemical Dependents and Significant Others) in 1991[1] and a smattering of articles in journals and magazines, information about the extent of drug and alcohol use disorders among Jews is scarce. Most of what we know is anecdotal. This is what we do know: alcohol and drug misuse has not bypassed the Jewish community. We are far from immune. Synagogue worshipers may sip a little wine at Kiddush or even partake of some of the schnapps, but what they do at home, or with friends, or in the bar, or at work is not necessarily observed by the rest of us.

We hear our friends or acquaintances whisper about so and so whose husband or wife or son or daughter has developed a drug problem, and it feels like a dirty little secret, a source of shame and reproach, something best kept under wraps. But when enough of us have heard these stories, we start to realize that the problem may be more widespread than we had imagined. At this point, we are fooling ourselves if we think "Jews don't use." We now can admit that substance use disorders are probably as much a problem among Jews as in any other cultures.

As long as the Jewish community held on to that myth, the more aware among us could accuse the rest of being in denial. Now that the myth itself has been debunked we face a new problem. Jewish law distinguishes between the two categories of *zadon* (willful, intentional transgressions) and *shegaga* (unintentional transgressions). Naturally, willful transgressions are much more serious than unintentional ones. So until recently we may have fooled ourselves into believing that Jews don't use, and we may have done so *b'shegaga*, unintentionally, because we really believed it wasn't a Jewish problem. Nowadays, I don't think people believe that anymore. In this sense, the old myth has become a myth in itself; The fallacy that Jews don't use no longer

---

1   Vex and Blume, "The JACS Study I: Characteristics of a Population of Chemically Dependent Jewish Men and Women," Journal of Addictive Diseases vol. 20 (4), 2001; 71-89.

holds water, and we can no longer fall back on denial or unwillful ignorance to justify our inaction.

Today we confront a newer challenge: Since we know that addiction indeed *is* a Jewish problem just as it is in other cultures, our inattention and inaction take on the aspect of *zadon*. Now we become guilty of a willful commission of the sin of indifference. We are in violation of the commandment in Leviticus, "Do not stand idly by the blood of your fellow," (Leviticus 19:16). Taking their cue from this verse, our Sages taught us that if we see someone drowning or under attack by robbers or a wild beast we are obligated to try to rescue him.[2] Moreover, we are warned against withholding evidence in a criminal case if we can testify in favor of the accused (e.g. Leviticus 5:1). Failure to do so constitutes a willful transgression.

We might think of the person with addiction as the one accused. It is as if he were sitting in a courtroom in front of a judge, feeling ashamed and guilty for a series of wrongs. We become potential witnesses who are summoned to give testimony on his behalf. We realize we have a choice: either to rise to his defense or keep silent. We know we can offer testimony that will buttress his case. We understand that addiction is a disease that no one consciously desires. We empathize with his suffering for we are aware that he has been overtaken by his addiction and is now feeling trapped. But as long as we keep silent and fail to stand up for him we are withholding vital evidence. We are the ones who turn into witting transgressors while the innocent yet accused sufferer is condemned for the "crime" of being addicted.

What does it mean to rise in his defense and offer testimony? This question will be discussed in Part Two, but for now let's settle with the adage "knowledge is power" and admit that the dawning of understanding about addiction leads to positive actions and the saving of lives. Until knowledge and understanding are embraced, we remain in the darkness of inaction. The spiritual fog of addiction engulfs not only the addicted but those of us who recognize the problem but remain inert.

---

2   The Sages' views on the obligation to rescue are summarized in Maimonides' law code Mishneh Torah, Nezikin (Torts): Laws Regarding Murder and Preservation of Life 1:14,16.

Chapter 2

IN THE CLOSET

In the 1980s and 90s, as the HIV/AIDS epidemic did its damage, the fog of ignorance and intolerance prevented victims from coming forward to seek help. Society's homophobia and condemnation of IV heroin users framed the intolerance. Gays remained subjects of discrimination within the American legal system and were often ostracized by their families, co-workers and places of worship. Not until June 2015, by an act of the U.S. Supreme Court, did same-sex marriage become legal by federal law. Even now, undercurrents of homophobia remain strong in some circles.

Back in 1987, while so many people were dying from AIDS, the US Congress under President Reagan banned the use of federal funds to support AIDS education and prevention. As a result, those who were vulnerable to the virus were left to suffer. American society's attitudes, at least on government and institutional levels, remained shrouded in darkness and prejudice against gays and people with addiction.

The tides began to turn when famous people started admitting that they had been diagnosed with HIV, or when they were dying of AIDS, and some of them were heterosexual. The intolerant among us started to care more when we realized that the epidemic wasn't confined to IV heroin users and gays. The more enlightened among us continued to struggle for the rights of the LGBTQ population and applauded when effective medications such as AZT became widely available. Societal attitudes combined with availability of treatment caused a major shift in the prognosis for people with HIV. As more of them learned to live with the virus instead of dying from it, more of the vulnerable felt encouraged to come forward to get tested. Many lives were saved, and the crisis abated.[1]

The parallels between the HIV/AIDS crisis and the opioid

---

1   For a concise summary of the sifts in attitudes about HIV/AIDS see Gwendolyn Barnhart, "The Stigma of HIV/AIDS," *In the Public Interest Newsletter,* American Psychological Association, December 2014, https://www.apa.org/pi/about/newsletter/2014/12/hiv-aids.aspx

epidemic, as well as the addiction problem in general, are remarkable. The spiritual fog of addiction engulfs both people with addiction and outsiders; The former may feel discouraged from seeking help because of their deep sense of shame, and the latter persist in endorsing stigmatizing ideas. The shame of the sufferer comes from a feeling of failure as he absorbs outsiders' moralizing judgments. No wonder he stays hidden. He cannot bear the idea that his "failure" will be exposed to ridicule and condemnation. He would rather suffer in silence than go for help and support. He may be afraid that his family and friends will look down on him once he confesses his problem, especially if he had been hiding it effectively from others.

Meanwhile, the outsiders persist in wielding the hammer of morality and judgment. Why is this? Think, for a moment, about the meaning of the term "homophobia." The last part of the word is defined as an extreme or irrational fear; some people avoid or discriminate against gays to this very day because they fear what they cannot understand. When this was such a prevalent attitude in decades past, the harm committed against the LGBTQ community was immeasurable, culminating in the multitude of deaths resulting from AIDS. When we consider addiction and other mental illnesses, the phobias continue be concealed behind the mask of morality and judgment.

Here are a few examples. Jack has been in recovery for almost a year. When he attends his family's Passover Seder, a cousin whom he hasn't seen in a long time greets him with, "So Jack, are you still using that shit? When are you finally going to stop?" The underlying message is: Jack is weak-willed, seen not as a whole person but as an addict. I wouldn't blame Jack if he felt like crawling out of the room.

Phil is a patient in a residential treatment program for substance use disorders. The program requires total abstinence and Phil follows the program rules, attends all groups and individual therapy, cleans up after himself, is considerate of others. He finally earns a day pass and goes to visit his parents. He feels uncomfortable while spending several hours with them because he senses their own discomfort. He begins noticing that he is experiencing some cravings. He uses the tools he has learned in treatment to "urge surf" through the cravings until they subside.[2] But they don't. Near the end of the visit he

---

2   Urge Surfing is a tool commonly used in cognitive behavioral treatments for relapse prevention. See Sunjev K Kamboj, Damla Irez and Tom P. Freeman, "Ultra-Brief Mindfulness Training Reduces Alcohol Consumption in At-Risk Drinkers: A Randomized Double-Blind Active-

surreptitiously finds his way to the liquor cabinet and downs a few shots of whiskey, heads to the bathroom to use some mouthwash, chews some mints and bids goodbye to his parents. Upon returning to the treatment program, he is given a breathalyzer test and blows a positive number. The director summons him into his office and proceeds to kick Phil out of the program.

Residential and outpatient programs have the right to follow an abstinence based model like this if they so choose. Indeed, most residential programs need to proscribe all drug or alcohol use by their patients. But there ought to be a little leeway if someone falls momentarily off track. In the case cited above, by forcing Phil to leave the program, the director is refusing to treat the very symptom that brought Phil there in the first place: his struggle with drug and alcohol cravings. Moreover, his slip involving a few drinks of whiskey is actually a symptom in itself. Yet hasn't he sought out treatment in order to get help coping with this very symptom?

Let's imagine that you have diabetes and are receiving treatment from an endocrinologist. During an appointment the MD informs you that your blood sugar levels are too high. She asks if you have been watching your diet. You tell her that you've been going to Dunkin' Donuts lately and overdoing it on the jelly donuts. Does the MD have the right to kick you out of her practice for exhibiting symptoms of your disease, namely for acting on your cravings for sugar? Similarly, I believe treatment programs err when they eject a patient who, by having a slip, exhibits the very symptom of the disease for which he is being treated. There are exceptions. Unlike Phil, if the patient is in full relapse mode, he may need to be removed from the treatment milieu to preserve the safety of the other residents. But to make him leave after one slip? Isn't this an overreaction that shows a lack of understanding, empathy and compassion for the one who is struggling to get well?

One more example of the unfortunate tendency to moralize and judge: Jane has decided to seek treatment for a severe opioid dependence. She attends an outpatient clinic that provides her with Medication Assisted Treatment (MAT) including daily dosing of methadone plus group and individual therapy. As part of the treatment protocols she is expected to show up at the clinic every day except Sunday for her medication (she receives a take-home bottle on

---

Controlled Experiment," *International Journal of Neuropharmacology*, November 2017: 20(11). http://www.ncbi.nim.nih.gov, p.4.

Part One – The Spiritual Fog of Addiction

Saturday) when she stands on line in front of the dispensing station and drinks a cup of juice with the methadone mixed in while the nurse observes. She is required to give a urine sample, attend groups, stay current with her Treatment Plan by meeting every 90 days with her counselor. Outside of treatment, Jane attends Narcotics Anonymous (NA) meetings at least 3 times per week.

She is doing well in her treatment. But she is having some issues with her 12 Step program. She has told her NA sponsor that she takes methadone, but she doesn't share this with anyone else at meetings. She knows that, because she is receiving MAT, she is not entitled to chair meetings or hold certain service positions. She has heard the NA message that she is not considered "clean" until she is methadone-free. She wants to be considered "clean" and a successful, leadership-quality member of her 12 Step fellowship. So Jane is in a quandary: Either taper off the methadone before it is considered medically safe to do so, thereby putting her at increased risk for relapse and even OD, or stay on the methadone but feel like a second class citizen in her NA fellowship.

What underlies Jane's quandary is the 12 Step program's persistent stigmatizing of MAT, suggesting that as long as Jane is taking methadone she is still an addict, that she has simply replaced one addiction with another. Her sponsor and NA friends are confusing her physical dependence on a medication that supports her recovery with a distorted notion that such dependence is really an addiction. They confuse *medical* dependence (like methadone, insulin, certain psychiatric medicines) with *chemical* dependence (addiction to illicit or drugs and alcohol).[3] The result is a confused woman who wants to keep getting better but is caught between two conflicting models of recovery. She has become a victim of well-meaning but misguided individuals who, though recovering from addiction themselves, have become harsh critics of the way she wants to regain her health.

Just as with the HIV/AIDS example, people with addiction will feel more encouraged to come out and seek help once society changes its attitudes and practices tolerance and acceptance. Until this happens, the sick and suffering will remain outside the door, reluctant

---

3   "Principles of Drug Addiction Treatment: A Research-Based Guide (Third Edition)", National Institute on Drug Abuse, January 2018, https://www.drugabuse.gov/publications/principles-drug-addiction-treatment-research-based-guide-third-edition/frequently-asked-questions/there-difference-between-physical-dependence

to ask for admittance to the very realm that may save their lives. The fog of addiction does not only settle upon those who are addicted; It engulfs those of us who remain unaware and unwilling to change the intolerant attitudes that repel those who are seeking help.

In the next chapter we will try to understand how and why individuals, families and communities continue to be resistant to positive change in attitudes about addiction.

Chapter 3

EYES WIDE SHUT

I believe Jewish families and communities share a deeply embedded resistance to opening our eyes to the true nature of addiction and recovery. How did this come to be?

Let's go back over a century to the days of first-generation Jewish immigrants to America from Eastern Europe. While "greenhorns" were looked down upon by "established" American Jews, this helped motivate the immigrants to try harder to assimilate. Diaspora Jewry has long been characterized by its chameleon-like ability to merge and assimilate into host cultures. In America, this historical and cultural trend took on remarkable proportions.[1]

Here are just a few among a countless number of examples.

In 1893 a five-year-old boy left his native Russia with his cantor father and mother and immigrated to the United States. Just eighteen years later in 1911, Israel Beilin penned a song that would soon become an international hit, "Alexander's Ragtime Band," and the long, storied career of Irving Berlin took off. Only through some type of alchemy could a young Russian Jewish emigrant capture the burgeoning soul of a country as it became the major world power after World War I; Berlin would assume the role of a kind of American cultural ambassador to the western world. He became even more American than people who were born in America. Berlin was always at the cutting edge of whatever defined American culture. Who could have guessed that a native Yiddish-speaking Jew from Russia would eventually be the composer of "White Christmas," "Easter Parade" and "God Bless America," a song that would become a second national anthem after 9/11? Berlin's amazing gifts of composing tuneful music and clever lyrics in the English vernacular may have been uniquely his own. But they symbolized something far greater: an immigrant Jewish culture that mysteriously would become as American as apple pie.

---

1   See Irving Howe, "World of Our Fathers: The Journey of Eastern European Jews to America and the Life They Found and Made," (New York and London: Harcourt, Brace Jovanovich), 1976.

In 1917, Abraham Cahan, the editor of the Yiddish newspaper Jewish Daily Forward published his landmark novel "The Rise of David Levinsky." This novel told the story of a young Jewish immigrant from Russia who rose from poverty on New York's Lower East Side to become a wealthy, Americanized businessman. In doing so, he sacrificed his cultural and religious identity, as well as his integrity and happiness. Though a fictional account, unlike Irving Berlin's biography, Levinsky's rise symbolized the erosion of Jewish identity and the dear cost of "making it" in America.

In the early 1960s, the great American Jewish author Saul Bellow wrote a review in the New York Times of a reissue of "Levinsky". While praising Cahan's realistic and effective portrayal of early 20th century American Jewry, Bellow wrote that Cahan "had a remarkably good head about the self-interest, snobbery, social climbing, money and the Americanization of the Jews."[2]

These two cases illustrate the success story of Jews in America. Bellow's quote offers an insight not only into the psyche of 20th century American Jewry but also into the world view that has sidelined the addiction problem for many decades. Our forebears achieved the "American Dream," but the cost was dear. Jewish identity eroded and many Jewish communal infrastructures saw a decline over the years. Jewish religiosity and spirituality were overshadowed by the ideal of financial and social success. In Chapter 7 I will discuss the shifting pattern of Jewish identity and how it relates to individuals challenged by addiction. In the present context I am interested in how fealty to the American Dream has affected our *spirituality.* By spirituality, I refer to the *interconnectedness* among people and the bonds between ourselves, God and the natural world.

Thus, an achievement and success orientation can pose a severe threat to spirituality because, in the spirit of cutthroat competitiveness, it can sever connections within the human family and that can foster addiction.

My personal story is an example. Like so many American Jews, I was bred for success. Luckily for me, I possessed enough natural talents, ability and drive to achieve my goals. But there are many of us who are less fortunate. They are the ones who are more vulnerable and susceptible to developing addiction disorders. If you add genetic and environmental wiring for mental illness to the mix, the risks of

---

2   Saul Bellow, "Up From the Pushcart; The Rise of David Levinsky," *New York Times Review of Books,* January 15, 1961.

becoming chemically dependent increase considerably.

I was raised in a loving, stable home in Connecticut. I attended a Conservative synagogue for Hebrew School and became Bar Mitzvah there. My only Jewish hook was my love of synagogue liturgy, and I was active in my beloved Cantor David Leon's (z"l) teen Sheirut Group where I volunteered to take assignments reading Torah and leading the congregation in prayer. Otherwise, I was turned off to Jewish practice and never active in youth groups. I dropped out of Hebrew high school after only one year. I continued to drift away from Judaism in my later high school and college years, only to begin finding my way back via the study of Judaism and post graduate years of study in Israel.

In other words, I was a pretty typical Americanized Jewish kid of the 50s, 60s and 70s.

Throughout my childhood, my parents would often talk about my future as a lawyer. When people would ask me about my career goals, I would always answer that I wanted to become a lawyer. When I entered college, I planned to major in political science with the idea of eventually going to law school. Something shifted in my sophomore year and I became interested in the study of cultures and primitive religion. In my junior year I encountered the Bible on a scholarly level for the first time and I was hooked. For me, law school was now out of the picture.

During my time in Israel as a graduate student I became interested in learning more about *Halakha* (Jewish Law) and observance. I began experimenting with some ritual behaviors. Then I decided to try wearing *tefillin*.[3] A friend of mine showed be how to put them on. I was intrigued, even a little excited. So in one of my weekly aerogrammes to my parents I asked them to ship my Bar Mitzvah *tefillin*. I can only imagine how my mother must have reacted, having been raised in a totally non-observant home and never having been given a Hebrew name or Jewish education. My father was raised in a modern Orthodox home but had essentially left most Jewish

---

3   *Tefillin*, often translated as "Phylacteries" (!), consists of two black leather boxes containing small parchments with verses from the Torah. The boxes are placed on the upper part of the forehead between the eyes and upon the upper arm on the non-dominant hand, and they are attached to the head and arm by means of black leather straps that hang down from the head and are wound around the arm and hand. *Tefillin* are worn every morning during prayer with the exception of Sabbaths and holidays.

observance behind. All in the quest to be fully Americanized. And now here was their son, studying thousands of miles away in Israel, asking for his Bar Mitzvah *tefillin*. What were they to make of this?

Now imagine how my parents felt several months later when I informed them of my decision to enroll in rabbinic studies at the Jewish Theological Seminary. The plan had been for me to become a lawyer, and now they had to absorb the reality of their son the rabbi! My career choice was inconsistent with my family's values; though they were highly ethical, kind and good people, they came from – and held on to – a strong belief that to be successful one must have significant wealth. Eventually, my parents grew very proud of their son the rabbi and loved to brag about me to whomever would listen. They were especially delighted when they would run into my congregants who were kind enough to share positive comments about me.

My story is atypical in certain respects but it reflects common American Jewish attitudes about success and achievement in the 20th century. I broke the mold in my family by entering the rabbinate, I made a career choice that struck family members and friends as quite odd. Yet I too was partly driven by the values with which I was raised. After ordination I served a small congregation in Columbus, Georgia, then moved to a medium sized synagogue in Wayne, New York and eventually landed in a large congregation in Woodbridge, Connecticut. I felt motivated by the desire to be the rabbi of a large synagogue, earn a good salary, enjoy the prestige that comes with such a position. In this sense I combined my spiritual and religious proclivities with standard American Jewish notions of what it means to "make it."

As I was growing up, I observed the "self-interest, snobbery and social climbing" that Bellow spoke of all around me. I also realized that those unhealthy attitudes have sidelined those whom Jewish society considers the *schleppers,* the ones who lag behind, underachieve or fall off the grid of social acceptability. I never felt this way about my career choice; my parents eventually embraced my rabbinic persona, and I often felt honored and appreciated by my community. But the part of me that rejected American Jews' success and achievement orientation helps me to understand the sense of alienation and failure experienced by people with addiction. I may have chosen an unusual career path for a "nice Jewish boy," as the old joke goes, but I believe I attained a position of honor and respect in many circles. Those who suffer from chemical dependence are the outliers who rarely attract positive attention or even compassion among fellow Jews, those same people who label addicted people as failures.

Not only do our Jewish cultural values help engender a competitive spirit that leaves so many behind, but our community continues to close its eyes to the plight of people with addiction. Synagogues rarely provide space for 12 Step meetings. To my knowledge, Jewish Federations and Family Services do little or nothing to fund addiction education, prevention and treatment initiatives. This baffles me. Since biblical times we have set our sights on aiding the widow, orphan and stranger in our midst. Nowadays we show sympathy for those afflicted with diseases such as cancer, heart and lung ailments, auto-immune diseases and many others. Most of us would admit that addiction is also a disease, but at the same time we choose to ignore or stigmatize it. We do the same thing with certain mental illnesses like mood and personality disorders and psychoses. All these types of mental illnesses, including addiction, can cause erratic, unpredictable and disturbing behaviors that can lead to isolation. Family, friends and co-workers may decide to keep their distance from the person with mental illness and addiction precisely because of those behaviors. After all, who wants to associate with someone who can be untruthful, selfish, unreliable? Clearly, this is not how we react to the cancer or Lupus patient. There are diseases, and then there are diseases.... The ones that stir our compassion tend to be the ones (like cancer or heart ailments) that don't generate the troubling or anti-social behaviors.

One further reflection on a community that shuts its eyes to those afflicted with addiction: The social pressures and fierce sense of competition that have driven American Jews for over a century can leave the ones who lag behind in a quandary. For surely not all of us can keep up. Those who can't compete and prevail in the game of success may choose to sit on the bench and turn to drugs. Others may be so caught up in winning the game that they use drugs as a pressure release valve. Either way, once the benchwarmers continue to sit out the game, they are subjected to the stigma of a judgmental, intolerant community made up of the winners and cheerleaders among us. We grow uncomfortable with people who can't or won't play the game the ways we expect them to. Some of them opt for a different game and pursue less competitive options. The Jewish sanitation worker or custodian may feel very proud of building a stable life and a solid home and family, but how many parents brag about their son the custodian or their daughter the house cleaner? Not everyone can complete medical or law school. Not everyone can build a successful business and earn a big salary.

Those who are overtaken by alcohol and addictive drugs may feel overlooked or scorned by the rest of us. We are part of the American Jewish success story; they feel like they have failed us and themselves. The sense of oblivion offered by psychoactive drugs becomes a welcome salve to the people who simply have not been able to compete and achieve. The American Jewish community of the last century has set the bar high. The ones who have supposedly fallen short are left behind to cope with their feelings of embarrassment, shame and failure. Once they have fallen into addiction they are alone. And the rest of us, the "winners" and success stories, talk out of both sides of our mouths. We may be "generous" enough to claim addiction is a disease while we shut our eyes to the sufferers who never wanted the disease in the first place. We say we embrace the medical model of addiction but we treat people with addiction like pariahs and moral weaklings. It is time for our community to take a hard look at this.

Chapter 4

MEDICAL VS. MORAL

As I wrote earlier, the Moral Model of addiction is alive and well.[1] It ought to have been put to rest and buried long ago. The Moral Model has its roots among the "Bible thumpers" of the past who focused on those Biblical passages in the *Tanakh* (Hebrew Scriptures) and New Testament that emphasized the evils of excessive imbibing. The Temperance movement of the 1800s leading to the establishment of Prohibition in 1920 was an example of this kind of religious moralizing. The person who could not control his drinking was considered morally weak. He lacked the will power to either drink moderately or abstain altogether. The Moral Model viewed alcoholism as a state of abject spiritual corruption and sinfulness. Those who held this belief did not distinguish between the drinking person and the behaviors resulting from his drinking. If the behaviors were anti-social and objectionable, the drinker became an object of scorn and derision. The guy named Joe who happened to have a drinking problem was talked about as Joe the alcoholic, a failure and weakling who was of little use to society.

The advent of Alcoholics Anonymous in the 1930s had a revolutionary impact. One of its most notable contributions was its rejection of the Moral Model in favor of a Medical Model of alcoholism. This new movement spoke of alcoholism as a disease and frequently described the excessive drinker as "sick". According to the AA philosophy his drinking was a result of his powerlessness over alcohol resulting from a sickness, not a pattern of bad, weak-willed choices made by a sinful individual.

The "Bible" of Alcoholics Anonymous (AA) – (often referred to as the "Big Book") included in its preface a section called "The Doctor's Opinion," in which a prominent physician specializing in treatment of alcoholism, Dr. William Silkworth, outlined an early

---

1   For a further explanation of the Moral Model versus the Disease Model, see Al Leshner, "Addiction is a Brain Disease, and It Matters," *Science* 1997;278:45–47.

Medical vs. Moral

version of the Medical Model.[2] He described the effects of alcohol on chronic alcoholics as a "manifestation of an allergy." The person who is unable to control his drinking has developed an allergy to alcohol and must avoid it altogether. As I would tell my patients in the clinic, someone who is allergic to peanuts cannot eat them at all. The consumption of even one peanut could be catastrophic. For the person with alcoholism who is trying to abstain from alcohol, even one drink could lead to disaster.

But what if this isn't always true?

The older versions of the Medical Model like that posed by AA and Dr. Silkworth left no room for the Harm Reduction Model that allowed for the possibility, though perhaps uncommon, that a person in recovery could be able to move from chronic, excessive drinking to moderate or light consumption. I believe that the Medical Model has evolved. Addiction may be thought of as a disease or condition in the sense that it has a cause, a progression and an outcome. If untreated, it may progress into severe physical and emotional impairment that may lead to death. But with medical interventions, the progression may be arrested. Does that necessarily mean that the patient may never touch a drink or drug again without falling back into the abyss? Not necessarily.

In my clinical experience I noted many cases of patients in recovery who were benefiting from treatment and fulfilling the goals of their Treatment Plans while still using limited or moderate amounts of their drug of choice. For one who holds on to Dr. Silkworth's type of the Medical Model, this may be hard to believe or accept. The old thinking would condemn the light or moderate user to a dire outcome. Anyone who claimed to be able to reduce his drinking from 12 to 2 beers a day would still be considered an active alcoholic who just happened to be drinking less. The old form of the Medical Model was an abstinence-based approach that left no room for any psychoactive drug or alcohol use by the recovering person.

But I witnessed something different during my years working in the outpatient clinic. I saw people who cut down on their use and held to that level indefinitely; alternatively, I saw others who cut down and eventually stopped altogether. Of course, there were those who fit Dr. Silkworth's model and, after reducing drug use without achieving abstinence, would inevitably escalate and return to previous levels of

---

2   *"Alcoholics Anonymous,"* Third Edition (New York: Alcoholics Anonymous World Services), pp. xxiii-xxx.

excessive consumption. However, I'm interested in the cases of those who chose not to totally eliminate their use yet still made progress in treatment. They reported significant changes in their patterns of drug or alcohol consumption. At the same time, they were getting jobs, repairing family relationships, becoming more emotionally stable and experiencing improvements in their physical health. I saw people who shifted from downing a quart of vodka a day to an occasional beer while presenting with marked improvements in appearance, speech and cognition. Sometimes they eventually stopped altogether and sometimes they fell into full-blown relapse. But for the moment, they were benefiting from their own individualized brand of recovery.

Going back to Dr. Silkworth's identification of addiction with allergy, we can learn something useful by considering one further aspect of food allergies. Think about the difference between food allergy and food intolerance. According to the Mayo Clinic,[3] someone with the former will suffer a severe and possibly life-threatening reaction if they eat any of the food in question. So they must avoid it at all cost. Someone with the latter may be able to consume small amounts without any reaction. Or he may even be able to take a pill that prevents a reaction. For example, he may take lactase enzyme pills if he is lactose intolerant and avoid gastric distress after eating a dairy product.

The lesson is easily applied to addiction. The AA member whose life was saved by the program will readily admit that he cannot ever touch a drink. He may stand up at a meeting and say, "I'm Mike and I'm an alcoholic. I've been sober for 30 years. But I know that when I leave this meeting, if I decide to turn left out of the building instead of turning right to go home as I plan to, I could wind up at the neighborhood bar and I'll be sunk. So I'll never feel totally safe and I know I can't ever drink again." Mike is an example of Dr. Silkworth's allergy to alcohol.

But Mike doesn't represent everyone who has a drug or alcohol problem. Like the person with lactose intolerance who takes a pill and is able to eat a little dairy food, some people have a type of drug or alcohol intolerance that has causes them difficulties.[4] Take Bill,

3   James T. C. Li, "Food Allergy vs. Food Intolerance: What's the difference?" https://www.mayoclinic.org/diseases-conditions/food-allergy/expert-answers/food-allergy/faq-20058538

4   The use of the term "drug intolerance" may be counterintuitive because "tolerance" generally refers to the user's need for more of the

for example. Bill realizes he has a problem but if you ask him, he will tell you the solution is not necessarily to avoid that drug or other drugs altogether. In fact, he might not be ready to totally swear off his drug of choice. Since Bill has an intolerance rather than an allergy, an immediate solution could involve cutting down on his drug use if he doesn't want to abstain completely. In the short term this will reduce the harm effected by the heavier use and possibly, in the long term, lead to abstinence. Bill is able to achieve these goals by means of the treatment he is receiving, and he gets ancillary support by going to 12 Step meetings. These interventions are like the lactase pill that allows the lactose intolerant person to occasionally indulge in dairy products. Treatment can work, even when total abstinence is not achieved, even when abstinence isn't even the goal.

With all this talk about addiction, I believe it is important now to suggest a definition and explanation of the term. To begin, there is no consensus on the meaning of addiction. The medical and mental health circles have officially labeled addiction as a *disease* since the early 1960s. Nowadays, some researchers and scientists prefer to call it a *condition*, others suggest a medical approach that moves beyond the disease concept into a combination of autonomous choices and brain changes that lead to chemical dependence.[5] I am not a scientist or researcher; my expertise is derived from years of clinical work as a rehabilitation counselor plus decades of rabbinic service. Through all this I have found a definition of addiction that I prefer and that makes the most sense to me and the patients with whom I have worked.

According to the National Institute on Drug Abuse (NIDA), "Addiction is defined as a chronic, relapsing disorder characterized by compulsive drug seeking and use despite adverse consequences."[6]

---

drug in order to get the effect he wants. I am using the term in this context merely to point out the analogy between drug use and food consumption.

5   One notable example is Maia Szalavitz' excellent volume *Unbroken Brain: A Revolutionary New Way of understanding Addiction* (New York: Picador St. Martin's Press) 2016, in which she suggests that addiction is best understood not as a brain disease but as a type of learning disorder. The works of neuroscientists Marc Lewis and Carl Hart also present an alternative to the Disease Model that represent new trends in the scientific and medical understanding of addiction.

6   "Drugs, Brains and Behavior: The Science of Addiction," National

Part One – The Spiritual Fog of Addiction

In my clinic I often led psycho-educational groups and one of the topics I came to enjoy teaching most was Biology of Addiction. Initially, I was scared of the topic because I was never a science type. In fact, I dropped out of a biology course in college and signed up for an oceanography class to meet my science requirement. But as I continued to run this particular group at the clinic, I became increasingly comfortable with the subject, largely because the NIDA definition made sense and was easily accessible to myself and my patients. Though newer theories offer alternative and sound ways of understanding addiction (c.f. footnote 5 earlier), the Disease Model as described by NIDA always seemed to resonate with my patients.

As I taught the groups, I would break the definition into three parts. I'd often begin with the third phrase, "despite adverse consequences." I would ask the group members: "How many of you were able to continue using drugs or alcohol while managing to fly under the radar, to avoid harming yourselves or others? How many people can keep up excessive use and function normally? There always has to be some kind of harmful results that happen." I would present the group members with the fictional case of Mary who is told by her doctor during a physical that her liver enzyme levels are severely elevated because of her excessive drinking. The doctor informs Mary that she needs to stop drinking or she may be heading towards serious liver disease. After the appointment is over, she goes home and immediately proceeds to pour herself a large glass of wine. She knows that her drinking is harming her, but she keeps up the behavior despite the consequences. She does this because she is addicted.

I would then move back to the first phrase in the definition, "…a chronic, relapsing brain disease…" I would talk about the meaning of "chronic" as opposed to "acute" and describe the nature of a chronic condition, often comparing addiction to diabetes or obesity as diseases that can be lifelong and that no one consciously chooses. I would ask the members: "When you were a child and someone asked you what you want to be when you grow up, did you ever say, 'I want to be an addict?'" Then I'd explain how "relapsing" is not necessarily a life sentence or a hopeless condemnation. The risk of relapse can exist even for someone who has had years of recovery, though not for everyone. As I understand it, the inclusion of the word "relapsing" in the definition points to the preconditions for the addiction diagnosis

---

Institute on Drug Abuse, https://www.drugabuse.gov/publications/drugs-brains-behavior-science-addiction/drug-misuse-addiction

Medical vs. Moral

itself. "When you first came to this clinic," I would point out, "when you had your evaluation, the clinician asked you whether you ever tried to stop using on your own and whether you had previous episodes of treatment. Most of you said that you made several attempts to stop and had other treatments before coming here." Frequently, people reach the addiction/chemical dependence/severe substance use disorder diagnosis after multiple efforts to change the behaviors until they realize they need to try a new treatment.

Staying on the relapse idea for a little while longer, I would mention the oft-used adage, "relapse is part of recovery." I'd say, "I know lots of people use this statement, but I don't really like it very much. I understand that it is intended to mean that if you relapse it doesn't have to be permanent, you're not necessarily back at square one, you learn some lessons and get back to the business of recovery. The problem with this is that you all know that relapse can be catastrophic, even fatal. So it's better not to think of it as part of recovery. Instead, as I see it, *relapse is a symptom of the disease of chemical dependence.* So if you relapse we're not going to kick you out of the program. We will treat the symptom and help you to get back on track."

When it comes to the brain disease idea, I also like the word *condition*. Either way, we are talking about a problem that has a cause, a progression and an outcome. I would discuss the process of neurotransmission and how psychoactive drugs mimic the brain's natural neurotransmitters that, once they lodge into the neuron receptors, will register sensations of euphoria, sedation and well-being. Then, moving on to the second phrase of the NIDA definition, "... compulsive drug seeking and use," I'd explain how tolerance effects the need to take more and more of the drug and how withdrawal sets in if the drug becomes inaccessible. Both tolerance and withdrawal play significant roles in the compulsive drug seeking and use, and the thrill of the chase after drugs can often be more exciting than the actual consummation.

Hearing all this, the group members would keep nodding their heads in assent and recognition. They may not all have known the words and concepts I was throwing at them, but they had the most powerful knowledge of all: the knowledge that comes from direct experience.

My Biology of Addiction groups usually featured what I called my pizza story. This parable captures part of the essence of the way addiction works on the mind. I'd begin by asking the clients to name

Part One – The Spiritual Fog of Addiction

their favorite pizza place (New Haven is famous for its thin-crust brick oven pizza). Then I would say, "Imagine you get up in the morning and get ready for a day at work. You don't really want to go in today, it looks like it's going to be a tough one, so you need something to look forward to after work that will help get you through. You decide that you will go to your favorite pizza restaurant X. Every so often, as the work day wears on, you think about the restaurant and the pizza and you cheer up. You now have something to look forward to. You finally leave work and drive to X. As you get near to the parking lot you see the red awning in front and you are already getting excited. After parking, you walk into the front entrance and start smelling the delicious aroma of hot pizza. The dopamine in your brain is getting all fired up in anticipation. You're lucky because you don't have to wait for a table. After sitting down and ordering, you notice that the people at the table next to you get served before you even though they came in after you did. You feel a little annoyed but you're willing to wait.

"Finally, the pizza arrives, piping hot, on a big tray placed in front of you and your companions. You're not feeling particularly considerate so you immediately help yourself before others get the chance. You might blow a few times on the slice but without waiting for it to cool you shove it into your mouth. You can feel it burning the roof of your mouth but you don't care. So there will be a little irritation up there for a while later, so what? You wolf down that first slice, you enjoy it, then you grab another and another. You still enjoy the second and third slices but not as much as the slices before. After a while you realize you've eaten 7, 8, 9 slices, and the later ones aren't as pleasurable as the earlier ones, but it doesn't matter because you know you can't stop until you're so full you feel like your stomach is bursting."

After finishing the parable I'd ask the group members for their interpretation, especially for their ideas on how this story is a metaphor for addiction. They always came up with the right answers, everything from the compulsion to use that gets one through the day, the thrill of the chase, the excitement caused by those dopamine chemicals going wild in the brain, the use of the drug despite harmful results (like burning the roof of the mouth), the initial thrill that is replaced by semi-automatic impulses to keep consuming even though the enjoyment is no longer there. One of the big differences between pizza and drugs, I'd point out, is that it would be exceedingly rare for someone to die of a pizza overdose. My pizza story illustrated

Medical vs. Moral

for my patients how addiction functions in the brain and how bad it feels when the drug isn't immediately obtainable, just as the story's main character would have felt had he pulled up to restaurant X and realized it was closed for the day.

Hard to believe, but not everyone loves pizza. Not everyone loves or engages in drug use. The way we are wired genetically, plus early childhood, learning, past experiences as well as specific associations can determine whether we like pizza or any other food, whether we like sugary or salty things, whether we are prone to obesity, whether we like uppers or downers or no drugs at all, whether using a particular type of drug will lead to our becoming addicted. Dr. Nora Volkow, the Director of NIDA, takes pains to compare obesity with chemical dependence.[7] No one chooses either condition. They just happen, often beginning with a series of bad choices and culminating in a medical condition that will only be arrested with the proper kind of treatment. Moral strength or weakness have little to do with it, neither does a person's ethical goodness or lack thereof. Once we are wired in a certain way, we can decide whether or not to get help. But the wiring itself is not of our choosing.

---

7   Nora Volkow, "Why Do Our Brains Get Addicted?" TEDMED video, January 2015, link is found online: https://www.drugabuse.gov/about-nida/directors-page

Chapter 5

NOT OUR FAULT

The fog of the Moral Model is evident in the way family members, especially parents, take on guilt and responsibility for their loved ones who have fallen into addiction. "What did we do wrong?" is the attitude at play here. "How could we have let this happen, why didn't we prevent it?" The very notion that good or bad parenting can cause or prevent addiction is a moral judgment. I'm all for morality, but not when it comes to the question of how and why addiction happens. I'm all for the Jewish value of providing the kind of parenting that inculcates in our children love of Torah and our fellow human beings. But I am acutely aware that all our fine efforts to raise solid, healthy Jewish children can hit a rock-solid wall when confronted with addiction and mental illness.

The spiritual fog of addiction disorients parents and family members who wrongly believe they are at fault when a loved one is overtaken by addiction. This doesn't occur out of poor oversight, neglect or other deficiencies among parents, spouses, siblings or friends. Yet I often hear people lament their inability to stop the juggernaut of addiction from affecting their loved ones.

I served as a congregational rabbi for 35 years. My wife and I raised two children who are now adults. We provided them with a good Jewish education, Jewish camp, a kosher, observant home. Both have distanced themselves from their Judaism. Is it our fault?

Some might say we should have done more to fortify our children's Jewish identities. But I know my wife and I did our best. Surely there were things we could have done differently, but the outcomes would probably not have been much different. Is parental guilt called for here?

I believe the same holds true in the case of raising children who eventually suffer from addiction, depression or other mental health problems. In the world of Al-Anon (the 12-Step program for people who have been affected by addicted loved ones) the operative rule of family responsibility is called the Three C's: "We didn't **C**ause it. We can't **C**ontrol it. We can't **C**ure it."

The first "C," we didn't cause our loved one's addiction: I have known fine parents, Jews and non-Jews alike, whose children developed severe drug or alcohol dependence in spite of the good upbringing they received. Parents, siblings and spouses don't cause their loved ones to fall into addiction. This is something we Jews have trouble grasping, as smart as we may be. Perhaps this is partly because we struggle with our own brand of Jewish guilt, a propensity for assuming responsibility for the perceived failure of those closest to us.

I believe Jewish guilt may have its own cultural features, but we don't own guilt any more than other cultures or religions. We just do it in our own uniquely Jewish way. This can play out when Jewish parents beat themselves up when their children don't turn out according to "plan." Especially when they wind up suffering from addiction. We parents blame ourselves. We wonder if we could have prevented it, if only we had raised them differently, if only we had been better parents, if only....

No one fully understands the causes of addiction. But this I do know: the causes are complex, and it is too tempting to attribute addiction to bad parenting. Parents don't turn their children into diabetics. Or asthmatics. Or schizophrenics. Or addicts. If Jewish parents can let go of their guilt, it may fade and they may be able to get on with their lives and find happiness and serenity. And in so doing, they will ultimately be more helpful to their children.

The second "C", we can't control the addiction or the resulting behaviors: No amount of meddling on our part will determine whether the drinking or drugging stops. Hiding the bottles, discarding the drugs may buy a little time but won't solve the problem. Cajoling or nagging won't either. Neither will enabling, which may be a *particularly* Jewish talent.

The myth of Jewish parents spoiling their children, like all myths, is grounded in truth. It starts when we feel bad about standing by without intervening while our babies do what babies do: cry. It continues into childhood when we give them what they ask for without expecting them to honor our values and rules. Once they become adults, we make excuses for them. We may do these things out of love or guilt, but whatever we do will not necessarily determine what they do.

If they become addicted, we can be supportive and compassionate, or practice tough love and set firm boundaries. But however we relate to them, we cannot control their addiction. Much as we would wish, we cannot force them into sustained recovery.

There's a saying in Al-Anon rooms, directed to those affected by another's drinking: "Don't just do something, sit there!" This is hard for Jews. We are a culture that venerates action, intervention and control. The idea of passively watching a loved one self-destruct from drinking or drugging feels wrong to us. Especially in the wake of the Holocaust, after much of the world stood idly by while six million Jews were slaughtered, a "never again" mentality drives us to resist inaction while others suffer, especially our loved ones. But this is precisely what is often called for after we realize that the pattern of involvement, control or enabling is doing more harm than good. Because addiction is a progressive, potentially fatal disease, controlling and enabling can be Jewish ways of killing with kindness.

Which brings us to the third "C." Contrary to 12-Step philosophy, I believe addiction *can* be cured. Or at least it can morph from a chronic relapsing disease into long-term, sustained remission. Either way, the cure or recovery won't happen primarily because of outside influences.

As parents or concerned loved ones, we don't engineer the cure. Jewish parents love to take credit for our children's successes – and we are prone to take responsibility for their failures. The success of long-term recovery comes about not from parental interventions but through the addicted person's own motivation and commitment to change, often in combination with some good treatment and self-help/peer support like 12 Step or faith-based programs. As loved ones, we can support and encourage. But we cannot control or cure the disease.

The limits of parental influence have ample precedents in the Bible. Starting with the story of Adam and Eve, we already see that God's first children go their own way regardless of God's directive against eating from the Tree of Knowledge of Good and Evil. Adam and Eve are unable to prevent Cain from murdering his brother Abel. The entire generation of the Flood is wiped out because of its rebelliousness. Abraham has trouble regulating Ishmael. Isaac and Jacob have their own issues with their children. As for Moses himself: The great prophet and lawgiver couldn't control his own family or people. His brother and sister complained about him behind his back. His people Israel built a Golden Calf while he was on Sinai receiving the 10 Commandments. They kvetched throughout the 40 years of wandering in the desert. And what could Moses do about it? Not very much, other than to keep focused on his mission, know his limits and stay in close communication with God.

The Bible is replete with examples of God's powerlessness over God's children. God has high expectations of the Israelites; they are called the Chosen or Treasured People (*Am Segulah*), they are charged to become a light to the nations (*Or la'goyim*). God wants the Jews to sign up as partners in bringing the knowledge and acceptance of the one God to all the peoples of the earth. And what do they do, time and time again throughout Biblical history? They violate the Covenant, they worship idols, they ignore God's commands. The God of the Bible is repeatedly exasperated, even angry at the rebelliousness of the Jews. Yet God promises never to completely cut them off. God's love, compassion and tolerance will always prevail, and the people are always given more chances after failing. The Bible understands the nature of people and posits that the nature of God is merciful to the core.

Parents, especially parents of children with addiction, can take heart from this Biblical message. The Biblical God doesn't cause, control or cure God's children's contrary or maladaptive behaviors. These behaviors always involved breaches of morality or ritual. Even God couldn't stop the people from sinning, even though God tried to do so by imposing punishments and granting rewards. So too are parents limited in managing their children's behaviors and lifestyles, inside and outside the sphere of morality. The Bible often refers to the stiff-necked and immoral qualities of the Jews; God simply can't do very much about that no matter how many punishments they suffered. When it comes to addiction, which is *not* caused by immorality or weakness, parental influence can only go so far. Parents can and should teach their children to be good. They can try to teach them to be clean and sober or to avoid abusing drugs and alcohol, but there are no guarantees.

A leader and role model as great as Moses couldn't control or cure his people. The God of Israel constantly lamented the heedlessness of the Jews. We lesser mortals shouldn't expect to have equal or better results with our own family members. We would do well to keep this in mind the next time we start feeling guilty about our loved ones' struggles with addiction.

Judaism places a clear obligation upon parents to be teachers of their children. When we recite the Shema daily, we are reminded *"v'shinantam l'vanekha,"* "teach your children (words of Torah)," (Deuteronomy 6:7). A section in the Talmud (Kiddushin 29a) lists a father's obligations towards his sons including *brit milah* (ritual circumcision), *pidyon ha-ben* (redemption of the firstborn), teaching Torah and a craft and to get him married. The obligation to teach his son how to swim is mentioned as well. The reason given is that the child's life might depend upon it.

In other words, with the exception of the two rituals at the beginning of the list, parents are obligated to provide their children with the tools for independent, productive living. Teaching a child to swim is an example of basic survival skills. But what happens when a parent feels he or she has done all these things yet the child drifts into a life of addiction in her teenage years? Every good effort has been made, hardly a stone has been left unturned in the quest to make this child a *mensch*, but for reasons hard to fathom, the child falls off track. The parent beats him or herself up, wallows in regret and self-doubt about perceived failures in parenting while the child goes merrily, or haplessly, along a path of her own choosing.

Indeed, Judaism offers a solution and a powerful insight to those anguished parents. In the Midrash (Bereishit Rabba 63:10) Rabbi Eleazar ben Shimon taught: "A man is responsible for his son until the age of thirteen; thereafter he must say, 'Blessed is He who has now freed me from the responsibility of this boy.'" All those parents out there who continue to feel shame and reproach, often self-induced, ought to thank Rabbi Eleazar for this valuable statement. Children up to age 13 were not considered obligated to observe the *mitzvot* designed for adults. Also, unlike adults, children who committed wrongs did not bring sacrifices to the Kohanim (priests) during Temple times and were not expected to do *Teshuvah* (Repentence) in the conventional way. The parents were expected to guide, teach and discipline their children and were held partly responsible for the children's transgressions. But once the child had become Bar or Bat Mitzvah, the parent could no longer be considered liable when the child went off track, transgressed, missed the mark. The parent would no longer be held responsible for the child's actions. The father would praise (Hebrew *barukh*) God for this kind of absolution. God would represent the force that allows the father to let himself off the hook and stop beating himself up for the "sins" of the child.

The statement suggested by Rabbi Eleazar appears more verbose in the English translation than it really is in the original Hebrew:

Not our Fault

"*Barukh she'petarani me'onsho shel zeh,*" literally translated as "Blessed (is He) who absolves me from the punishment of this one." The statement is a type of formula and indeed has become a declaration that is formally recited by some fathers when their sons become Bar Mitzvah. The formula doesn't even have the courtesy of referring to the son as "this *son*" or "this *youth,*" it simply refers to the boy as "this one," almost as if he isn't worth mentioning by name. Rabbi Eleazar acknowledges that human beings who have reached the age of adulthood (age 13 in his day, equivalent to perhaps age 18 in our time) may do things that are beneath human dignity. Translating this notion into today's reality, teens and young adults may fall into a life of addiction that carries along all the unseemly, degrading behaviors that ensue. A child who brought joy and *nachas* to his parents is now shooting up heroin or snorting cocaine. He may be going to dangerous parts of the town or city to procure drugs. He may be stealing from his parents or others to support his addiction.

Lamenting all these behaviors, the parents will ask: How did this happen? Where did our wonderful child go? Rabbi Eleazar would caution them: You did your best, you imparted your values, you served as good role models. But now that your child is old enough, you need to let go and let the chips fall where they may. You are no longer directly responsible for all that happens to your child.

Naturally, there are exceptions to this. Children living in their parents' homes need to abide by the family rules. Parents ought to do their best to enforce these rules. That is often almost impossible, especially with acting-out teens. When matters become extreme, when lives are at risk, when the teens are indulging in patterns of behavior that may imperil their healthy maturation and growth, parents need to intervene. But after the parents have stepped in and done their part, if the results are disappointing or worse, they have to learn self-acceptance, and self-forgiveness.

We would do well to heed the timeless wisdom of the great mystic Kahlil Gibran described in his seminal book "The Prophet":

"Your children are not your children.
They are the sons and daughters of life's longing for itself.
They come through you but not from you.
And though they are with you, yet they belong not to you.

You may give them your love but not your thoughts.

For they have their own thoughts…

You are the bows from which your children
   as living arrows were sent forth.
The archer sees the mark upon the path of the infinite,
and He bends you with his might that His arrows may go
   swift and far.

Let your bending in the archer's hand be for gladness.
For even as He loves the arrow that flies,
So He loves also the bow that is stable."[1]

    Gibran wrote that God loves both the flying arrow (the child) and the stable bow (the parent). This is a helpful reminder, for it is often hard for the parent struggling with an addicted child to remain stable and strong, and it is also sometimes hard for that parent to feel the love toward the child that God feels. That parent may feel continually tested not only by his child but by God as well. Nevertheless, whenever the parent reminds himself, or is reminded by others, of the need for some healthy detachment and self-forgiveness, a great burden is lifted off his shoulders.

    The fog of the Moral Model persists whenever the struggling parents indulge in self-recrimination and blame. These are the attitudes that can bring chronic sadness and depression. It is normal for the parents to wonder whatever happened to that sweet, loving little boy or girl who had so much promise and potential. And it is normal to lament the loss of a dream that, at least for now, appears to have been thwarted. But perseverating over such feelings of sadness and loss can only bring helplessness and a kind of spiritual paralysis. The Medical Model, instead of the Moral Model, rightly adjusts the parents' attitudes and helps them to realign their sense of responsibility. They didn't cause, can't control, nor can they cure their child's disease of addiction.

---

1   Kahlil Gibran, *The Prophet* (New York: Alfred A. Knopf, 1923), p. 17.

Chapter 6

OUR MORAL INSTITUTIONS

The Moral Model is still entrapping our Jewish communal institutions. The spiritual fog of addiction prevents these institutions from seeing clearly the problems of addiction and the needs of those who are suffering. I see this happening in four ways. First, consider the paucity of synagogues that host 12 Step meetings, indicating a refusal to see addiction as a Jewish communal concern. Second, consider the pervasiveness of 12 Step approaches in Jewish treatment programs, as if the Steps have been elevated to Sinaitic authority. Third, some Jewish experts are directly addressing or treating the addiction problem while expressing resistance to Medication Assisted Treatment (MAT). Fourth, as our once vital institutions erode, it becomes easier for the affected individuals or families to slip into invisibility and remain hidden.

By now you have surely seen that I have some ambivalence about 12 Step programs. My reservations stem from some of the programs' attitudes towards MAT and Harm Reduction approaches. But by and large, I continue to be impressed with the extraordinary results of self-help programs like AA and NA. Countless numbers of people have claimed that the fellowships have saved their lives. They attribute their sobriety to their Higher Power, the efficacy of the 12 Steps and their adherence to the principles of the program. Not everyone is inclined to follow this path, and I believe the Jewish culture needs to promote alternatives both within the treatment and self-help worlds.

Nevertheless, it would behoove our community to do its part in making 12 Step programs more accessible to our members. Few synagogues and JCCs open their doors to 12 Step meetings. I'm sure there are some congregations in more urban areas that host meetings in their buildings but I have the impression that they are few and far between.

Picture the following scenario: A synagogue board of directors is asked by a member or the rabbi to consider housing an AA meeting. Here are some of the comments and objections raised at the board meeting:

"I don't want a bunch of alcoholics and strangers in our building."
"How will this possibly benefit our synagogue?"
"I don't want those people coming anywhere near my kids."
"There aren't too many Jewish alcoholics, this isn't a Jewish problem."
"Most of them aren't Jewish, let them go to a meeting in a church."
"They don't belong here."
"What if they disrespect our building?"
"What if they steal from us?"

Many 12 Step meetings are held in churches. Many of those meetings end with the recitation of the Lord's Prayer. This has contributed to the myth that alcoholism and addiction are gentile problems. For most synagogues and JCCs, the possibility of welcoming 12 Step fellowships and their members is remote at best. Thus, there is an institutional bias within the Jewish community against people with chemical dependence. I believe that the board discussion would be quite different if the synagogue were to be approached by someone wanting to establish an Overeaters Anonymous chapter, or perhaps even a Gamblers Anonymous chapter. But renting out a room to a bunch of "addicts" or "alcoholics" seems ill-advised to the average Jewish lay leader. That is because the Moral Model still holds sway.

Going back to the board discussion, I am certain that the objections raised above happen in churches as well. Yet when meetings are held in religious institutions, those institutions are almost always churches. The scarcity of 12 Step meetings in synagogues is one further example of how the Jewish community overlooks the chronic problem of chemical dependence.

Perhaps I am being too harsh on those board members. Maybe I am being unfair to our brethren. Bear in mind, this is a hypothetical situation and the discussion is a collection of typical statements by those who stigmatize people with addiction. I would love to be proven wrong about this. I would be delighted if the problem I am highlighting doesn't really exist, or that it exists only minimally. Unfortunately, I have the strong impression that I am not overstating the problem.

But I might be wrong, or at least partly wrong in one respect: More than likely, the scenario itself hardly ever happens anyway. How often do rabbis petition their boards to welcome 12 Step meetings in their houses of worship? How often does a courageous synagogue member ask her board or rabbi to begin opening their doors to meetings? As a personal aside, I have, over the years, contacted rabbinic colleagues and offered to speak about addiction in their congregations. Especially since the opioid crisis escalated, I considered it important to provide education and awareness to synagogues. The result has been disappointing. The requests for lectures have been few. Rabbinic colleagues whom I have known and respected have responded to my offers either by putting me off or by not responding altogether. In either case, the passivity of many of my colleagues is baffling to me. Their inaction speaks volumes about the shame and stigma attached to addiction. In the wake of this public health epidemic, all congregations should be addressing the problem in some way. How dare they shut their eyes? I only hope those colleagues who refrained from inviting me decided to confront the crisis in another way that is equally or more effective than bringing me in to deliver a lecture.

If my hypothetical board meeting scenario were to occur more frequently, at least this would create opportunities for education and enlightenment, both for rabbis and laity. I pray that synagogues and other Jewish communal institutions will begin to see the value of hosting 12 Step meetings. After all, is it not the Jewish way to support healing and recovery for all those who suffer from disease, including addiction? It is certainly not the Jewish way to turn our backs on their affliction.

I have noticed a dichotomy between Jewish institutional exclusion of 12 Step programs and the prevalence of 12 Step approaches within Jewish addiction treatment circles. Synagogues and JCCs may avoid providing space for meetings, but almost every Jewish treatment program I know includes 12 Step recovery models as a central part of treatment. This has become de rigueur over the past few decades. Perhaps it stems from the pioneering work of Rabbi Abraham Twersky and other luminaries who have successfully demonstrated the consistency between the 12 Steps and Jewish teachings.[1]

Still, I find it curious that this approach has become so widespread in the Jewish treatment world. The 12 Step philosophy represents the recovery path for those who are involved in self-help, peer support fellowships such was AA and NA. But the 12 Steps are not treatment per se; they are not evidence-based, nor are they proven to be *medically*

---

1   Some examples include helpful books by Rabbis Kerry Olitsky, Rami Shapiro, Paul Steinberg and Mark Borovitz.

effective. But it seems to me that they have become *Torah Mi-Sinai*, as if they possessed the authority of the Torah given on Sinai.

I'm sure the 12 Steps as incorporated into treatment have helped countless numbers of Jews in recovery. Though the long-term outcomes may be elusive, I would guess that the short-term outcomes have been largely successful. But I contend that the 12 Steps, whether as an adjunct to treatment or as strictly self-help outside of treatment, are not the only way and may not work for everyone, as I discussed in my Introduction.

Secular minded Jews who eschew God talk may be turned off by the prevalence of God and Higher Power in 12 Step fellowships. They may try attending meetings and if they voice reservations about the God or Higher Power talk, they will hear canned answers like, "If you don't believe in God, let the fellowship be your Higher Power, or pick any Higher Power you want." That may be well and good, but one cannot avoid the intrusion of God near the very beginning of the Steps (Step 3: "Made a decision to turn our will and our lives over to the care of God as we understood Him."). This can be an irritant to people who are sincerely seeking recovery but are not interested in going the God or faith route, or any route that combines spirituality with God orientation. They may be open to spirituality and its impact on rebuilding relationships with others while tapping into one's own inner spiritual power. But they'd rather accomplish this without having to affirm God or constantly listening to the faith-based affirmations of others.

I would like to see Jewish treatment circles make way for alternative approaches outside the 12 Steps. SMART Recovery[2] (a self-help program that is non-faith based and relies on cognitive behavioral principles) or *Mussar* (a movement stressing ethical and spiritual growth developed by Rabbi Israel Salanter, a 19th century Lithuanian rabbi) combined with evidence-based treatment that does not disguise itself as self-help would be a welcome development.

This leads me to one of my greatest concerns about the way we provide treatment: a baffling tendency to (here's that word again!) stigmatize medical therapies that have been proven effective. This concern has to do with the omission of MAT in Jewish residential treatment centers along with vestiges of ignorance related to opioid

---

2 More information about SMART Recovery is available on the program's website, https://www.smartrecovery.org

maintenance therapies among so many of our population, including medical professionals. Were I a journalist, I would probably want to conduct interviews with treatment professionals in Jewish outpatient and residential programs and ask the following questions: Do you provide MAT in your facility? If not, do you offer transportation to MAT providers for your patients? If the answer to these questions is NO, does this reflect a policy in your program? If so, what is the philosophy behind your policy? How do explain your policy's compatibility with the Medical Model of addiction?

Studies and research over the years have affirmed the long-term efficacy of methadone maintenance therapy. Buprenorphine has only been utilized for opioid dependent patients during the past 15 years, so the studies re: long-term outcomes are as yet inconclusive, but signs indicate positive and beneficial results. Methadone is an opioid agonist that binds to the brain's opioid receptors and reduces cravings and withdrawal symptoms. Buprenorphine is a partial agonist medication that also binds to the opioid receptors with a ceiling effect, that is, anything over a certain ceiling dose will have no effect. The results are similar to methadone; cravings and withdrawal symptoms are reduced or eliminated. Naltrexone is an opioid antagonist that blocks the effects of all opioids. All medications are approved by the FDA. All are recommended by addictions specialists for patients with moderate or severe opioid use disorders.[3]

So I continue to wonder: considering the *medical* benefits of MAT, why do Jewish treatment providers resist it? How can this resistance be reconciled with the Medical Model of addiction and treatment? The answer eludes me. Part of the reason may have to do with the influence of 12 Step fellowships' bias against MAT along with the misguided view that those receiving methadone or Suboxone (the company name for buprenorphine plus Naloxone) are merely replacing one addiction for another. This along with the predominance of 12 Step approaches within Jewish treatment programs may help explain why more of these programs do not offer MAT options to their patients. But I suspect this is not the entire answer. There must be more to the picture. I'm just not seeing it.

In addition to the alternative models mentioned above (SMART,

---

3   The research studies that confirm the efficacy of methadone and buprenorphine for opioid dependence are too numerous to list here. Visit the NIDA (www.drugabuse.gov) and SAMHSA websites (www.samhsa.gov) for further information.

Mussar), I would like Jewish treatment programs to provide every opioid dependent patient with the opportunity to receive an assessment and evaluation to determine whether they are appropriate for MAT. This does not mean that every treatment center must have a methadone dispensary on premises or an MD who can prescribe Suboxone. It merely involves providing transportation to methadone clinics or MDs who are approved buprenorphine prescribers. The program itself can help monitor compliance and assign a staff member to administer these medications in order to prevent diversion. If the program is unwilling to follow these procedures, it ought to refer the patient elsewhere if she wishes. Jewish treatment centers are not obligated to endorse MAT. But they are obligated to make appropriate referrals for those who seek it.

It doesn't seem so difficult to make all this happen. The difficult part is working through the resistance so that the attitudes can change, the stigma allayed and the Medical Model enforced.

In October 2013 the Pew Research Center published "A Portrait of Jewish Americans."[4] The study generated lots of strong reactions among Jewish leaders, especially due to its findings about the decline in Jewish identity during the past few decades. I am not a demographer, nor am I a journalist who conducts extensive interviews, but I have some impressions about how the weakening of our communal institutions can impact the addiction problem.

In the past, when most Jews affiliated with synagogues and supported their local Jewish Federations, it was relatively difficult for Jews to slip under the radar, especially in smaller Jewish communities. After I was ordained in 1982, my wife and I moved to Columbus, GA, a small city with about 1,000 Jews, and I became rabbi of Shearith Israel Synagogue. At that time the congregation had some 150 families. The Reform congregation, Temple Israel, had approximately 180 families. Comparing the total number of the Columbus Jewish population to the total of affiliated families it is easy to see that the synagogue affiliation rate was very high. Almost every Jew in that city was known and identified. It was almost impossible for a "marginal" Jew to hide. During my six years in Columbus, rarely did a Jewish

4   Pew Research Center, "A Portrait of Jewish Americans," October, 2013, Found online at http://www.pewforum.org/2013/10/01/jewish-american-beliefs-attitudes-culture-survey/

name come to my attention that I hadn't heard of, unless the person was new to the city. As a result, Jewish identity was strong in that southern community, and the support system was solid. People with health problems were cared for, mourners were comforted, no one felt alone and isolated unless he chose to.

I recall a few people who were struggling with mental health, drug or alcohol problems. They felt welcome in the synagogue and did not feel compelled to avoid attending services out of shame or embarrassment. As far as I know, they did not feel ostracized or judged by their peers.

The Columbus, GA Jewish community was small, but strong and proud. The vitality of its institutions contributed to positive feelings of identification among its members. When this happens, and when Jewish anonymity is almost impossible to maintain, Jewish individuals rarely fall through the cracks. Those who begin to slip into the isolation caused by addiction and mental illness are usually noticed. If they wish to get help, they are encouraged to do so. If they prefer to struggle with their problems on their own, or even if they do not believe they have a problem, they are still welcomed and embraced for who they are.

Certainly, this is not always the case. I know I am speaking in generalities and from personal and professional experience. But I suspect that a tightly knit Jewish community, especially a small to medium one, will provide a warmer, more nurturing milieu for almost all its members, including those who have "issues". Today, many synagogues and other Jewish institutions are engaged in an existential fight just to stay alive. How will this affect those who are addicted? Other than 12 Step meetings, where can they go where they will feel comfortable and accepted? This may be one advantage offered by Jewish treatment programs. But the supports and resources are lacking in the community at large.

In the next chapter I will explore how the identity of the Jewish individual impacts vulnerability to addiction and whether a stronger identity can act as a deterrent.

Chapter 7

CULTURAL AND RELIGIOUS IDENTITY

In this chapter I will address the following questions: Does a strong Jewish cultural and/or religious identity help prevent addiction? Does the lack of a strong cultural and/or religious identity set up a higher risk for developing an addiction problem?

On face value, these questions might appear to be different ways of asking the same thing. But this is not the case. Each question calls forth different considerations, and the implications do not always converge. Unfortunately, a lack of thorough and definitive demographic studies on addiction in the Jewish community leads me to rely mainly on my own impressions and insights. So, as is often heard in 12 Step rooms, take what you like and leave the rest.

Turning to the first question, does a strong Jewish identity help prevent addiction? Some cross cultural studies have suggested that religion and cultural factors can play a major role in addiction prevention. A distinction ought to be made between teens and adults; for teens, sticking to protective norms of their cultures or religions decreased the likelihood of forming friendships with "deviant" peers. When they adhered to the customs and folkways of their faith groups they tended to avoid experimenting with illicit drugs.[1] For adults, evidence shows that religiosity can provide an increased sense of security and stability plus a higher degree of emotional and spiritual resilience based on faith. People who embraced their religious way of life were less prone to addiction, and people in recovery typically found their religiosity to be a vital tool in relapse prevention.[2] I need

---

1   Flavio Francisco Marsiglia, Stephen Kulis, Monica Parsai, "God Forbid! Substance Use Among Religious and Non-Religious Youth," *American Journal of Orthopsychiatry*, October 2005: 75 (4), pp. 585-598, found online at https://www.ncbi.nlm.nih.gov/pmc/articles/PMC3043382/

2   "Drugs and Devotion: Comparing Substance Abuse by Believers and Nonbelievers," DrugAbuse.com, found online at https://drugabuse.com/featured/drugs-and-devotion/

to emphasize that these studies focused on religions and cultures outside of Judaism. The scant research we have within the Jewish community seems to tell a different story.

The studies I have seen try to dispel common myths about the prevalence of addiction among Jews. For example, the JACS-commissioned survey by Vex and Blume (Jewish Alcoholics, Chemically Dependent Persons and Significant Others) cited above came to the following conclusions: earlier myths correlating chemical dependence with lack of education, income, and Jewish identity were debunked. Most addicted Jews were highly educated and high income earners. The survey also contradicted old presumptions that linked chemical dependence with alienation from Jewish culture and religion. The majority of respondents to the survey (59%) said they belonged to a synagogue, which is probably higher than the average Jewish population. Even more striking is the statistic that a majority of respondents remained active in social and religious Jewish life while active using their drug of choice (including alcohol). The authors of the study concluded that addiction is a bigger problem among Jews than previously known, and is not confined to religiously and culturally marginal Jews.[3]

I applaud all those involved in the JACS study and commend them for attempting to shed light on the problem of addiction among Jews. However, the study was based upon responses from people already in the JACS database and therefore reflects only a small cross-section of Jews with addiction problems. Those who were listed in the database were most likely people who self-identified as struggling with substance use disorders while professing an attachment to Jewish culture and/or religion. It would be nearly impossible to conduct a survey that would accurately report addiction trends among the general Jewish population. There are untold numbers who would never consider "coming out of the closet" about their addiction, or who have no idea what JACS is, or who would never respond to any questionnaire asking them about drug or alcohol use. So, we essentially wind up right back where we started, with little solid information to help us understand whether Jewish identity is an effective prevention tool.

Although the JACS study indicated that many respondents were synagogue members and had strong Jewish attachments, I don't believe this tells us very much about most Jews. The questions still

---

3   Vex and Blume, pp. 83-87.

remain: If someone attends synagogue regularly, participates in Torah study, has strong emotional ties to the state of Israel, is he at less risk for developing an addiction problem? If a teen is active in Jewish youth groups, goes to services occasionally, joins his family for Passover Seders, participates in Hillel in college and travels to Israel on the Birthright program, will she be less likely to fall into chemical dependence?

The answer is, I don't know. Perhaps someone will be able to use the tools of research and demography to study this thoroughly and issue a comprehensive report, but I don't really see this happening anytime soon. So, all I am left with are my impressions based on years in the pulpit rabbinate and the addiction treatment world. My sense is that a healthy Jewish identity may contribute to an immunity from chemical dependence but is no guarantee against addiction. Because the etiology of addiction is partly genetic and explained by the way the brain is wired, even practicing Jews are not entirely safe. Yet I believe that immersion in a life of Torah study and practice, and/or involvement in the Jewish community, and a devotion to *Tikkun Olam*, the repair of the world through social action, can all provide some safeguards against falling into addiction.

During my years in practice, I met with several Jews who were seeking help with their substance use problems. I recall that none of them were Jewishly observant or active in their community, but most if not all of them were proud of their Jewish heritage. They tended to feel connected to their cultural roots while experiencing an alienation from Jewish culture in the present. Though I was careful not to let my rabbi persona interfere with the counseling process, I sometimes asked them whether they had any interest in actively connecting with their Judaism. The responses were usually lukewarm so I didn't push the matter. I still wonder, had they been able to find their way back into active Jewish living, would this have improved their rehabilitation outcome? I will never know the answer to this. But I suspect that the building of positive Jewish experiences and a solid Jewish identity could be helpful in the prevention of addiction and, even moreso, of relapse once the addiction had taken hold.

A distinction must be made between how Jewish identity effects prevention on one hand and relapse prevention on the other. Because of genetic and psychosocial conditioning, factors like day school education, growing up in an observant home, attending Jewish summer camps and traveling to Israel may play some role in preventing addiction. This may be true especially when a person's identity formation and emotional stability are intact. The strong Jewish connections forged by these types of experiences can serve as a bulwark against maladaptive thoughts and behaviors associated with addiction. But again, there are no guarantees. I have known parents who have been baffled and upset when they provided everything they could in a Jewish way yet their children chose a different path. In fact, as I said earlier, I am one of those parents.

I will discuss in Part Two how the practice and study of Judaism can be a useful adjunct to treatment. In my view, Jewish practice is probably more effective in relapse prevention than in prevention of addiction itself because of biological and psychological factors. But this is only anecdotal and is not based upon any solid research that I am aware of.

Turning to the second question that I posed at the beginning of this chapter, does a lack of a strong Jewish identity present a risk factor for addiction? Once again, the hard evidence is scant. The Pew Study shows probably the best and most reliable evidence for a decline in Jewish identity during the last two decades. The research found that the number of self-identified Jews has declined by half since the 1950s, millennials are more secular than the previous generations (32% claim no religion and identify only on the basis of ethnicity, culture or ancestry), rates of intermarriage continue to increase (since the year 2000 some 60% of Jews have intermarried), Jewish observance is still declining. Two findings are particularly interesting: Jews tend to be less religious than the American public as a whole. Thus, if one believes that religion can be an effective tool in addiction prevention, one must conclude that the Jewish population is more vulnerable to addiction than other cultures and religions.

The other interesting finding has to do with the socio-economic status of American Jews. According to the Pew Study cited above, American Jews have a higher level of education and 25% have a household income of over $150,000 (only 8% of the general public have a comparable income). This shows that the bar for financial and educational achievement is set higher for American Jews. I understand this to mean that we put more pressure on our children to "succeed" than non-Jewish Americans do. Our view of success is mostly determined by money and professional attainment. When our children don't meet our expectations in these areas, they consider themselves failures. This sets up the psycho-social traps that engender addiction as well as depression and other mental illnesses.

American Jews tend to place a higher value on money and career over knowledge of Judaism and Torah. While this seems obvious and self-evident, it does say something significant. In the eyes of our community, when a strong Jewish identity accompanies financial and career success, that is all well and good. But given the choice between the two, most of us would pick the success card over the Jewish identity card. Torah knowledge is fine, knowing one's way around the Siddur is great, but the value system of our community inevitably lands on the dollar and the degree. Add to this the Pew Research data showing a decline in millennials' connection with the State of Israel and we wind up with a composite that is of concern not only for those worried about the future of American Jewry but, in the short run, for those who are worried about our children and loved ones' vulnerability to addiction and mental illness.

Over forty years ago when I wrote that aerogramme to my parents asking for my Bar Mitzvah *tefillin*, I had already been engaged in a process that was both physically, emotionally and spiritually restorative. For me, that process was necessary because I was trapped in a type of fog that was self-destructive throughout my college years.

The issue had to do with a lack of identity and self-differentiation. I'm not referring only to my Jewish identity; I'm pointing to a state of deep confusion about myself, my familial relationships, my place in the world. As it happens, I had little interest in Judaism during high school and the first three years of college. As I mentioned earlier, I thought I was cut out to be a lawyer. I also had a strong flair for music. I loved choral singing and I played guitar. By the time I got to college, I wasn't focused on either my hobbies or my career goals. I was involved in the drug culture as were many of my friends, but this was mostly limited to marijuana and hashish, and I did not develop a dependence on any drug. So I floundered around, performed well enough in my studies without excelling in any one subject.

Meanwhile, I became physically ill. I recall running on campus to avoid being late for a final exam during my junior year and suddenly feeing intensely faint. I was able to take the exam but afterward began to experience severe abdominal pain. I wound up in the ER and had to undergo some very uncomfortable tests (I will omit the details here). As it turns out, I was diagnosed with Crohn's Disease, an ailment that effects the digestive and auto-immune system. I recall being hospitalized a few times and receiving several pints of blood due to serious intestinal bleeding episodes. Eventually the symptoms would abate, partly with the aid of steroids and largely through the intervention of a wonderful gastroenterologist, Dr. Edward Grossman of Fairfield, CT.

I am aware that I had a genetic disposition for this disease because my mother began suffering from it while I was a child. Now, in retrospect, I believe that the Crohn's was really a symptom of something much deeper, a physical manifestation of a psychic, spiritual void that was chronically filled by stress and anxiety. I believe that the stress most likely contributed to my disease. As I existed in that spiritual and emotional fog through those years, I was unable to see a clear way out, to find a path towards health and wellbeing – until I discovered Judaism and went to Israel for the first time.

The state of fog and inner confusion that engulfed me 40 years ago is not unlike the experience of people with addiction. For Jews, the lack of a strong sense of religious identity can contribute appreciably to this spiritual fog or malaise. I do not suggest a necessary connection between Jewish involvement and risk of addiction. To say that a "marginal" Jew is more likely to become addicted is a tenuous proposition, especially given the scarcity of evidence to support this theory. Yet it is not a stretch to imagine that a person who is cut off from his Jewish state of being may exist in a kind of spiritual limbo or void. Drugs and alcohol can be convenient ways to help fill in that void. One thing can lead to another, and casual use or experimentation may eventually give way to dependence. The fog of identity confusion can mutate into the fog of addiction.

Chapter 8

THE SPIRITUAL FOG OF ADDICTION

I probably learned more about spirituality during my 10 years as an addictions counselor than during the entire span of 25 years serving as a full-time pulpit rabbi. The lessons I faced were harsh. The experiences of addiction in my family were a kind of trial by fire. I was able to draw from a fount of inner strength thanks to my faith, my spiritual director, my Jewish observance, a 12 Step program and especially my wife and closest friends. But my greatest teachers were my patients. They allowed me to hone my skills as a counselor, to test out some theories and to hear their perspectives. I have no doubt that, as many therapists have said in the past, our patients are our best teachers, as long as we are willing to humble ourselves and allow ourselves to be taught.

One of my most vivid memories of my rabbinical experiences happened shortly after I began my work at the small synagogue in Columbus, GA. Here I was, fresh out of the Jewish Theological Seminary, having completed many years of rabbinical studies, eager to go out into the world and teach Jews about Judaism and impart valuable lessons in life. I thought I was so smart and so wise for someone under 30 years of age. Then reality struck. I was thrown into a synagogue job, underprepared, somewhat lacking in practical training. Part of my job description involved serving as principal of the small religious school and teaching 6th and 7th graders. One of my 7th graders was a particularly challenging child, extremely bright, very sassy, quite disrespectful (or at least that was how I perceived her at the time – she was probably misunderstood by many adults). On one occasion she used an inappropriate word during class. After school I called her father to report the incident. When he heard my report he asked, "Was it a four letter word?" When I answered in the affirmative, he said, "Oh shit! Well rabbi," he continued, "you thought when you first came here you were going to teach us all this stuff about Judaism and life, but now it looks like we're the ones teaching you!"

A similar process happened to me when I became an addictions counselor and began working at the clinic. There I was, imagining I was some kind of hotshot rabbi, having led a large congregation in Connecticut, thinking that I had so much to teach and so many pearls of recovery wisdom to share. Once again, I had a rude awakening. My "rabbihood" meant little to most of our patients (though some were deeply respectful of anyone with a clergy title). I was just another middle age guy trying to run groups, trying to handle group members who were acting out, trying to just find some minimal level of effectiveness. I had to swallow my pride, tuck away my clergy status and become just Rick, a man who believed in recovery and who cared about those who were sick and suffering. And my patients became my teachers.

During my seminary years I learned a lot about religion, less about spirituality. During my full-time pulpit years I experienced spirituality largely through the lens of my congregants' joys and sorrows and my involvement in the most intimate moments of their lives. By "spirituality" I refer to the sense of interconnectedness between all things: people, nature, animals. To me, spirituality means the ability to draw from one's inner power, to understand that life has a purpose, to accept responsibility, to go beyond one's self in service to others, to stand grounded in one's self in a deep awareness of one's own needs and rightful place in the world.[1] Religion can help foster these things but, in my view, religion is not necessary to achieve spirituality. In my case, my Jewishness has been a partner with my spirituality. For me, I could not imagine one without the other.

So in order for me to become a better addictions counselor and a more spiritual person, I needed to find ways to learn from my patients. This goal would typically be realized during my experiences leading group therapy. In psychoeducational groups like Biology of Addiction, Relapse Prevention and Men's Trauma and Recovery groups I was charged with the task of providing education and insight to the group members and would enter the sessions armed with materials, theories and suggestions. All of this was useful. But the approach that was most valuable to me and my patients involved presenting them with questions, giving them the chance to share, trying to keep them focused on the group topic, listening attentively to what they had

---

1   C.f. a webpage called "Taking Charge of your Health and Wellbeing" on the University of Minnesota website, found online at https://www.takingcharge.csh.umn.edu/what-spirituality

to say, and then adding my own insights. Frequently, as I listened to them, a light bulb would flash in my mind and I would receive a fresh insight that I had not seen beforehand. These sessions served as a kind of learning lab for me as I would reveal my new insights to the members while keenly observing their reactions. If I noticed several heads shaking, I would ask them why they disagreed with me. I would learn just as much from this, maybe more, than from the instances when they agreed with me. When I observed several heads nodding, I felt that my insights were being validated. I would hold on to those new revelations and test them during subsequent sessions with different patients. If the heads continued to nod, that meant I was on to something. I was then free to incorporate these teachings into other group sessions, including one of my favorite group topics, Spirituality and Recovery.

Here are a few examples of spirituality lessons that I either discovered on my own or picked up from others but adapted successfully in the context of both group and individual counseling.

The first has to do with the concept of what I call the essential self. I'd explain to my patients that the essential self refers to who we really are deep down, the true essence of our personhood at its best, the conglomeration of all our fine qualities, our gifts, talents, our ability to care and empathize. The essential self entails positive human qualities and traits that animate – and are animated by – the human spirit. With the onset of addiction the essential self begins to recede. As the addiction continues to fasten its grip, the essential self becomes increasingly hidden within the fog of the compulsion to seek and use the drug of choice or, more accurately, the drug of necessity. This essential self becomes diminished by addiction, as the drug takes over and overshadows much of what is fine and good about a person. This happens not out of choice but out of necessity; the disease of addiction robs the individual of the freedom to make many positive, healthy choices.

However, as the fog of addiction thickens, the spark of the divine within the human soul is not extinguished. My patients always liked this idea and felt comforted by it. I would tell them about the "still, small voice" described by the prophet Elijah (I Kings 19:12), the inner voice of God dwelling within, calling upon the sick addicted individual to find health and recovery. This still small voice is analogous to the divine spark and both work in tandem, beckoning to the essential self inside the addicted person to reclaim itself.

How can such reclaiming occur? This will be addressed in Part Two and has to do in general with all tasks related to recovery and specifically with concrete and specific goals such as rebuilding family relationships, returning to work and resuming certain hobbies and interests that the patients had before becoming addicted.

The second trial balloon that worked consisted of a lesson in Martin Buber. It may be hard to picture a rabbi like myself talking about "I and Thou" to group members who never finished high school or spent years in prison or were still or had been engaged in prostitution. But, believe me, the presentation always worked.

Martin Buber was a German Jewish philosopher and sociologist of Judaism. He lived and taught during the first half of the 20th century, first in Austria and Germany and later in Jerusalem. He was born into a well-known family of Jewish scholars and became well known for his compilation "Tales of the Hasidim." Buber was naturally attracted to Hasidism, partly because of its emphasis on the immediacy and immanence of God. In 1923 he published "I and Thou," a philosophic work that influenced both Jewish and Christian theologians and is still considered one of the greatest books of theology of the 20th century.[2]

The first section of "I and Thou" is especially relevant to people with addiction because of its exposition on what Buber refers to as the world of "I-It," the world of common experience, where we engage with people, society and nature as objects to meet our needs, things to be utilized. We discussed how this relates to life in addiction, how the drug takes over one's life so that other people are reduced to becoming either a help or a hindrance for supplying the needed drug or drink. Former relationships are damaged or severed; drug using "friends" are really just acquaintances who will hang around when drugs are involved but will be otherwise absent. At critical junctures, most people with chemical dependence aren't really available for other people. They can't be, because the compulsive need for their drug of necessity does not allow room for empathic human responses. As a result, addiction makes it difficult to sustain relationships that are defined by empathy, friendship and love. Other people are reduced to mere objects of the addicted person's needs.

Of course there can be exceptions to this rule. Even in the addicted life it is possible to have moments of true relationship and what Buber refers to as dialogue. But the compulsions of chemical dependency

---

2   Martin Buber, *I and Thou* (New York: Scribner, 1958).

create obstacles to these types of experiences.

The patients in my groups responded very warmly to Buber's theory of I-It and even more enthusiastically to the phenomenon of I-Thou (which will be discussed in Part Two of this book). I recall one patient who was particularly interested. She was an African American woman in her 20s, whom I will refer to as R, in treatment for cocaine and phencyclidine (PCP) dependence. She was essentially homeless and had been engaging in prostitution. She was also not completely abstinent from drugs. She wanted to be in recovery and to stop using but her environment made this goal elusive.

The counselors at my clinic complained often about the challenges of treating PCP users and especially about their erratic and disturbing behaviors in groups. R could also be quite erratic. She was also highly intelligent. She enjoyed reading and like to talk about philosophy. So when I presented Buber's I-Thou approach, R appeared to be deeply moved. After the group session she waited behind to talk to me and she told me that Buber made a lot of sense to her. She said she was going to try to get ahold of the book. The following week, before group, she proudly showed me a volume of "I and Thou" that she had found at the New Haven Free Library. A few weeks later she reported that she had finished the book and really liked it. As for me, I was deeply impressed and sincerely happy that R, a woman with so many struggles and challenges, was inspired by Martin Buber. This taught me a valuable lesson: Inspirational teachings like Buber's, if they are true, clear and accessible, can transcend religions, cultures and socio-economic groups. Anyone can benefit from their wisdom. And anyone attempting recovery can find strength and hope in the truth of these teachings. R and Buber were but one example.

So far we have seen the fog of addiction described as the fading of the essential self and its entrapment in the I-It world. These connections made lots of sense with my patients. The third idea that worked for them was related to theodicy, the attempt to understand God's ways in the face of evil. Discussions of theodicy always revolve around the question of the meaning of suffering. During one of my spirituality groups, a patient asked the age-old question, refracted through the prism of one who suffered for years from the effects of addiction and mental illness: "Why does this happen to us? Why do we have to go through all this suffering and put other people through it also?"

After hearing this question, my initial silent reaction was, "Oy, here we go!" Actually, this is something I should have been prepared to answer. During my years as a pulpit rabbi I was frequently called upon to address issues of theodicy. My pastoral responsibility often required me to strive with the meaning of suffering and help my congregants through times of tragedy. The book that probably had the greatest influence on me, along with many of my colleagues, was Harold Kushner's *When Bad Things Happen to Good People*,[3] in which Rabbi Kushner taught us about the limits of God's power to prevent evil and the extent of God's ability to support people through suffering. I will never know how *theologically* sound this approach is, but I have long felt that it is *pastorally* useful. I applied Kushner's philosophy countless times when asked why God would seemingly allow bad things to happen to my congregants. I would explain that these things aren't part of God's plan and are not meant for some ultimate good. The usual reaction was one of relief. People didn't like the idea that they were being either punished or tested by God, so when they were told that God was doing no such thing most sufferers were at least somewhat mollified.

However, in the moment at the clinic when I was tested by one of my patients and asked about the meaning of his suffering, something new clicked for me. I understood that he wasn't one of my congregants and that my role was different here. I was now being called upon, during a group on spirituality and recovery, to help my patients sort out God's place in their addiction and their recovery. So I came up with a suggestion that I believed could work. I said, "I wonder if you guys are in a kind of special spiritual category, like you're being tested. Your addiction, or your mental health condition, is a kind of test that God is putting you through, and you're being given the chance to show your spiritual strength and courage by sticking with your recovery and refusing to give up on yourself." As these words left my lips I realized I was going out on a limb, but when I noticed all the heads bobbing up and down I knew my words rang true with my patients. One of the patients, not the one who asked the question, began to weep. He thanked me for the insight, he said that he was now able to feel that the anguish of his addiction and his mental illness had a higher purpose.

Why would they respond so positively to a theologically problematic notion like this? Wouldn't they, like so many of my parishioners in the past, reject the seemingly preposterous idea that

---

3   Harold S. Kushner, *When Bad Things Happen To Good People* (New York: Shocken Books, 1981).

the suffering of the righteous is part of God's plan to foster some greater good? Wouldn't they be inclined to divorce themselves from a God who would purposely cause suffering in order to test their faith?

The answer, I think, is deceptively simple. My addicted patients needed to feel special, somehow singled out from the rest of us, because *they are*! For some mysterious reason, God chose them to be wired for a mental health condition or disease that would cause them to feel isolated, ostracized and misunderstood. They experienced this condition as a test, a challenge to either meet or ignore. By meeting the challenge and striving for recovery, they were given the opportunity to tap into a deep inner spiritual power. Only addicted people could be given this special chance and rise up to prevail over such formidable obstacles.

As I continued to use this approach with patients, I realized that I was employing a kind of opportunistic, situational theology. As a pulpit rabbi I would minister to those experiencing tragedy or extreme grief and loss by reassuring them of the limits of God's power and the reality of their suffering as separate from any kind of imaginable divine plan. As an addictions counselor I would treat people with addiction or mental illness by reassuring them that perhaps God made them that way in order to single them out for the blessed task of recovery.[4] I suppose this sounds like I'm talking out of both sides of my mouth, maybe even contradicting myself, or being theologically inconsistent. But if practical theology is to be judged by its effects and benefits on the suffering individual, then I suppose I could be justified in presenting different, even opposing, views of God to different people depending upon their needs in the moment. In other words, whatever works....

When Rabbi Kushner wrote "When Bad Things Happen to Good People" in 1981 many rabbis and theologians considered it a radical departure from traditional Jewish theology because of the way he explained the limits of God's omnipotence. In truth, the book stood upon a firm foundation that was established by Jewish mystics like Rabbi Isaac Luria of 16th century Safed (in the Galilee, the northern part of what is now the State of Israel). Traditional Jewish theology would have rejected any attempts to impose limits on God's power to stop or prevent evil. Indeed, one of the most accepted notions of

---

4 To clarify: I would only bring up the topic of God when cued by the patient or while leading groups on spirituality. To do otherwise would have been unprofessional in a clinical setting.

God's role in human suffering was related to the Psalmist's statement "God tests the righteous," (Psalm 11:5). The following statement in the Midrash is attributed to Rabbi Jonathan ben Eleazar: "As a potter does not test defective vessels which would break with only one blow, so the Holy One tests not the wicked but the righteous (Genesis Rabbah 32:3)." Ever conscious of the Medical Model of addiction, we might think of chemically dependent people as righteous ones who did not choose their condition but are nevertheless made to suffer from it. For some unknown reason they are singled out by God, or by some random genetic selection if you prefer, to bear the burden of their disease.

The age-old concept of the Chosen People comes into play here. The Bible presents the Chosen People concept as a way of describing God's covenant and partnership with the Jewish people. Over the centuries, countless Jewish apologists have emphasized that the Jews were not chosen because of any inherent superiority over the nations. But it is obvious that the Jews have suffered greatly for over two thousand years, partly due to the fact of their very survival and uniqueness. This has led some to suggest that the Jews were chosen to suffer for their heritage; the Chosen People were singled out to endure persecution.

In a sense, people with addiction might be considered as if they were *chosen* or tested, singled out from among us to carry the terrible weight of a potentially fatal disease and given the opportunity to escape their plight through healing and recovery. But while they grope their way through the spiritual fog of addiction they experience the confusion, and even occasional terror, of living in darkness as they witness the absence of God in their lives.

Since medieval times, Christian theologians have written about the "dark night of the soul,"[5] a state of being when one feels spiritually empty and abandoned by God. God-believing Jews in the throes of addiction may acutely feel a kind of spiritual void marked by the absence of God. They are probably wracked with guilt for whatever they have done to hurt themselves or others. Their addiction has diverted them from the pursuit of a meaning-driven life. If they are observant and believe in the imperative of keeping the *mitzvot*, their compulsion to obtain and use drugs has gotten in the way of meeting their religious obligations. They may feel ashamed to appear regularly

---

5 E.g. a poem entitled "The Dark Night of the Soul" by John of the Cross, a 16th century Spanish mystic.

at synagogue or other public or family events. Plus, the regimen of daily prayer will be hard to maintain; Reciting the Hebrew prayers with any degree of *Kavannah* (intention, devotion) is almost impossible to do while under the influence of drugs or alcohol or while experiencing cravings or withdrawal symptoms.

Secular minded Jews may experience a similar kind of emptiness without using God language. For them, as well as for religious Jews, the void consists of a profound sense of isolation from family, community and society. Feeling cut off from family and close friends is especially challenging. Out of mortification, the family has a huge capacity for inflicting shame on the addicted person. His family and community sometimes send him into exile. They put him into a modern version of *herem*, banned and excommunicated, cut off from those whom he loves, unable to receive their support. His community identifies him as an addict. Not a person who suffers from an addiction but an addict, a label. The addiction takes the place of his personhood.

The isolated person suffering from addiction isn't talked about much in polite society. His absence is rarely noted at the Thanksgiving or Seder table. No wonder so many falsely believe addiction isn't prevalent among Jews! Those who do suffer are shunned, isolated, exiled and isolated. They are the forgotten ones, and the rest of us pretend they don't exist. In so doing, we help create the illusion that addiction isn't really a Jewish problem.

There are instances when it is necessary to set strong boundaries and to keep the addicted person at arms length or beyond. His actions can be too destructive or erratic for his loved ones to tolerate. In these cases, emotional and physical safety come first. But even with this understanding, shame about the person and circumstances persist.

The spiritual fog of addiction, like the thick clouds of actual fog, need not be permanent. The haze begins to lift once the person begins to take steps to change. As we will see in the next chapter, positive change often starts before any direct actions are taken. Individuals can change, so can communities, often as a result of shifts in attitudes and the decision to find healing and recovery.

Chapter 9

MOVING TOWARDS CHANGE

The Jewish community is in a state of denial when it comes to addiction, treatment and recovery. I have spoken to many Jewish physicians, psychologists and other mental health professionals who know little or nothing about MAT. They have asked me questions like: "Isn't someone on methadone still addicted?" I always try to answer them patiently, but each time I hide my frustration. I silently wonder when people will start to get it. If the professionals, who have been clinically trained and are supposed to keep up on the latest developments in science, medicine and treatment, do not understand the value of MAT, how can lay people be expected to understand?

Attitudes about addiction are reflected in the language that is used when discussing the topic. This becomes especially crucial during treatment in the way clinics and staff talk about the subject to their patients. But as I said earlier, the Jewish world as a whole needs to carefully examine the language of discourse about addiction and whether the language reflects an attitude of tolerance and acceptance.

I remember an instance when I delivered a lecture in a synagogue about the Jewish response to the opioid crisis and I referred to the HIV/AIDS epidemic of the 80s and 90s. I told the attendees that once society became more understanding and accepting about LGBTQ rights and stopped condemning those afflicted with the virus, more and more affected people became willing to stop hiding and seek help. One man raised his hand and said, "That isn't true. People became more tolerant when they found out it's not just a gay or heroin addict's disease, when Magic Johnson went public about it." He was, in effect, saying that most people are as intolerant as he is and will not be swayed as long as they can hold on to their narrowness. This same gentleman later raised his hand again and said that addiction is a matter of choice and willpower. Shortly thereafter he got up and left the lecture early. I didn't mind.

Just as the stigmatization of homosexuality and heroin addiction prevented people from seeking help during the HIV/AIDS crisis, the stigmatization of addiction among Jews creates a stifling, judgmental atmosphere. The words and concepts we use must be chosen deliberately and carefully if we are to foster an atmosphere of tolerance and acceptance. Otherwise we, even if we are well intentioned, can wind up unwittingly doing harm.

The way we use the term *Teshuva* is a good example of a valuable concept that can be easily misused and misunderstood. Here's what I mean: *Teshuva is* usually translated as "return" or "repentance." It can be viewed from two angles: as "repentance" it signifies a turning away *from sin*. As "return" it can indicate a return, or turning towards God. The latter is useful in the spiritual process of recovery. But the former can be deeply problematic.

Using the term *Teshuva* carelessly may actually discourage some from stepping out to reveal their disease and to seek help. It may inadvertently reinforce the false idea that addiction is a moral weakness or failure. Maimonides, in his code Mishneh Torah (Hilkhot Teshuvah 2:2), defines *Teshuvah* as follows: "What is *Teshuvah*? That *the sinner* shall give up *his sinning* and the *sinful man* his plans and inwardly resolve never to do these things again, as it is written (Isaiah 55:7), 'Let the *wicked* give up his ways...'"[1].

It is obvious that Maimonides, following the lead of the Bible and the Rabbinic Sages, understands *Teshuvah* as a spiritually healthy response to sin. Today, when we use (or overuse) this term in discussing addiction, we run the risk of being misunderstood. Connecting the *disease* of addiction to sinfulness is not the message we want to convey. Those affected by the disease, whether family or the ones with addiction themselves, may hear this message and decide to remain silent out of shame and fear of stigmatization.

Therefore, we need to exercise more caution when talking about addiction and *Teshuvah*. We ought to remember that sometimes in the process of trying to help people we may wind up harming them instead.

Teshuvah as a concept does have particular relevance to recovery, but in a limited way. It may be understood as a specific response to acts carried out by the addicted person during the acute stage of chemical dependence. His compulsion to use his drug of necessity may cause him to hurt himself and others. In order to move through recovery, he may begin to examine and inventory the harm he has committed and start to make amends. If he is part of a 12 Step program and is

---

1   Translation from Hebrew and italics mine.

"working the Steps" he will make a "fearless and searching moral inventory" and eventually "make direct amends" to others (Steps 4 and 9).[2] If he is finding a different recovery path he will still need to come to terms with the hurts he has committed in his addiction history. This is the meaning of *Teshuva* as turning *towards* God rather than *away* from sin.

Using language carefully, avoiding judgmental and stigmatizing words, will help foster an atmosphere of acceptance and tolerance. Once the Jewish community, including treatment professionals, grasps this fundamental axiom, addicted individuals will feel safer to admit their problem and seek help. Once the community shifts its attitudes, affected people will be more inclined to undergo positive change.

Individuals can change and so can communities. How does change occur? In late 1970s researchers James Prochaska and Carlo Di Clemente began developing a theory that came to be known as the Transtheoretical Model of Behavioral Change.[3] One of the key elements of this theory was the Stages of Change. The researchers were attempting to understand the nature and motivation for cigarette smokers who were considering quitting. The premise behind the theory was an acknowledgment that in order to help patients realize their goals of smoking cessation, counselors ought to know where the patients stood in their readiness to change. How deep was the resistance? What was the nature of the ambivalence? What was getting in their way? Without knowing these things, the counselor would run the risk of pushing a treatment plan that the patient wasn't ready for, thereby increasing the risk for failure.

Since this model was initially proposed, it has been extended for application to other types of addiction including alcohol, drugs, gambling sex and other problematic behaviors.

The Stages of Change are:

1. Precontemplation – The person may not be aware of or admit to having a problem and has no intention of changing his behavior.

---

2   Step 4: "Made a searching and fearless moral inventory of ourselves." Step 9: "Made direct amends to such people wherever possible, except when to do so would injure them or others."

3   James O. Prochaska and Carlo Diclemente, "Stages and Processes of Self-Change of Smoking: Toward an Integrative Model of Change," *Journal of Consulting and Clinical Psychology* 51(3), 390-5, July 1983.

2. Contemplation – He is becoming aware that he has a problem and is thinking about change but not in the immediate future (six months or so). The perceived benefits of the behavior outweigh the deficits.

3. Preparation – The person now knows that the problematic behavior has more cons than pros for him and is now intending to make a change in the near future (approximately one month). He is taking steps to investigate ways to implement the change.

4. Action – He has been involved in making changes during the past month or so.

5. Maintenance – The change has been in effect for about six months.

Since Part One of this book addresses the spiritual fog of addiction, I will discuss the first two stages here. The stages of Preparation and Action will be considered in Part Two and the Maintenance stage will be covered in Part Three.

I have found the Stages of Change model to be an invaluable tool in my counseling work. Assessments and evaluations and Treatment Plans assign a Stage of Change to the patient during set times along the treatment spectrum. Expecting a precontemplative patient to immediately begin changing would probably stimulate active resistance on his part. This has long been a problem in the field of human services. In this scenario the service provider, whether it be the probation officer, Department of Children and Families caseworker or addictions counselor would push her idea of whatever she thought was best for the patient. If the patient wasn't "compliant" he would be labeled "resistant." The service provider would feel frustrated, disappointed or angry at the patient, forgetting that the patient is really a person in his own right, one who probably knows what he can and cannot do and what he is willing or unwilling to do.

Until the last few decades, methods of counseling people with problematic behaviors often failed to consider the patient as a person. Not until the 1950s would the models of person-centered therapy pioneered by Dr. Carl Rogers and others begin to find their way into the treatment world, and it took many years before addictions treaters began to follow suit. In my view, many of us in the Jewish world still don't understand the value of these models. For example, we still think of addicted people as "addicts" rather than as human beings with a problem.[4] We still expect people seeking recovery to buy into 12 Step programs even if they aren't ready for total abstinence or are turned off by all the God talk. And we still talk about precontemplators as if they are "in denial," unwittingly declaring that we are somehow entitled to judge them and know what is in their best interest better than they can know themselves.

One of the reasons I like the term "Precontemplation" is because it is a kinder, more compassionate and non-judgmental way of describing what was once (and still often is) referred to as "denial." It recognizes that someone who has been engaging in problematic behavior may not be ready for change *yet*, but that the time may come. I am reminded of a story about the great 20th century German Jewish philosopher Franz Rosenzweig, the author of the "Star of Redemption." After growing up as a secular Jew and going through a period when he considered entering Christianity, he eventually embraced Judaism. Legend has it that he was once asked if he would regularly put on *tefillin*. His answer: "Not yet!"[5] This may be the answer of one who is in the Precontemplation or Contemplation stage of change. He may not be ready to change now, but that time may come. He just doesn't know it yet, or is not willing to admit it. **Pre**contemplation implies a present and a future; the present is of concern, usually to family and friends of the addicted person, but the future may possibly include positive change.

In addition to individuals, communities are always in flux, undergoing changes. I believe the Jewish community, if one may generalize, may currently be in the Precontemplation Stage of Change with regard to our understanding and awareness about addiction. As I have noted earlier, Jewish leaders in the field are still stuck in exclusively 12 Step models, as if they were the only viable options in recovery. On the other hand, how often do you see Jews at AA, NA or Al Anon meetings? For years as a practicing rabbi I would refer people to 12 Step meetings, most commonly to Al Anon when family members would seek my counsel. I can count on one hand the times

---

4   Notice that I have purposely not been using the terms "addict" or "alcoholic" in this volume. In doing so, I avoid using labels. Instead, I choose to use terms like "addicted person" or "individuals with addiction."

5   This legend is described in Louis Jacobs, "Franz Rosenzweig and the Founding of the Lehrhaus," *The Jewish Religion: A Companion* (Oxford: Oxford University Press, 1995).

they actually followed through with my recommendations. Though I have said, in a critical way, that the God/Higher Power orientation of 12 Step programs can be a turnoff to many secular-minded Jews, there are certainly many who could benefit from the programs but shy away, partly because of the God talk but mostly because of the powerlessness talk. For family and friends who are affected, this can be especially challenging; Al Anon advocates that people learn to mind their own business and stop controlling the addict or alcoholic. This runs against the Jewish grain. Aren't so many of us trained by our families to be in each other's business, to control and interfere with others? This becomes even more confusing when someone's lifestyle choices may be risky and even life threatening.

As I also noted earlier, the reluctance among so many of us to admit the benefits of MAT and to endorse programs involving methadone and buprenorphine is another example of our ignorance. It appears that many in the Jewish community are resistant to change in this area as well. We imagine that methadone is just another addiction, and we do so immersed in a fog of misunderstanding and judgmentalism.

Finally, we persist in telling ourselves that addiction isn't really a Jewish problem while inwardly perceiving the absurdity of this myth. In so doing, we become culpable for turning our backs on a problem whose gravity we must acknowledge.

So as I head toward the conclusion of Part One of this book, I am acutely aware of how easy it is to grow discouraged and depressed about the prognosis of the addiction problem in the Jewish community and among individual Jews. I have been talking about the spiritual fog of addiction and how it applies to addicted persons, their families, friends and communities. Enshrouded within that fog, it is difficult to see clearly, to hold some awareness of the nature of the problem and a view toward some solutions. However, things may not be as bad as they seem. If individual Jews and the Jewish community are in the Contemplative or even the Precontemplative Stage of Change, remember that change is still possible, even likely. Even precontemplatives are in a process of change, albeit at or near the beginning. Eventually, when addicted people and communities understand that the benefits of change may outweigh the deficits, that is when the scale will shift and positive change occurs.

Many of us in the addiction counseling field have been heavily influenced by the work of William Miller and his colleagues who developed a model called Motivational Enhancement Therapy (MET), also referred to as Motivational Interviewing (MI).[6] This is a short-term therapeutic approach to help patients find the motivation to stop engaging in harmful or self-damaging behaviors and to move toward positive change. The techniques and principles involved in MI are much too extensive to describe here. But a few things are worth noting: First, the counselor who has a preconceived notion of who a patient should be and tries to set the patient's goals based on this projection is likely to fail and is setting the patient up for failure as well. Instead, the counselor's role is to listen carefully and see where the patient is while helping him to develop intrinsic motivation for positive change. The power for personal growth comes not from the counselor but from the patient. Second, even if the patient sets a goal for positive change but shows some resistance, it is the counselor's role to see the resistance as an indicator that she may need to make some shifts and adjustments. The resistance may be a sign not of the patient's deficits but of the counselor's rigidity. At this point, the counselor may wish to try what is known in MI as developing discrepancy, or helping the patient to see the discrepancy between his goals and the behaviors that obstruct achieving these goals.[7] Working through an awareness of the discrepancy, the patient begins to experience increased motivation to continue moving in positive and healthy directions.

This theory is fully applicable to the challenge of how and when individual Jews and communities will find the motivation to begin emerging from the spiritual fog of addiction. As a rabbi, teacher and addictions counselor, I can choose to either take an argumentative stance, to cajole and persuade until I am blue in the face. Or I can choose to find ways to be a good listener, to better understand the pulse of the Jewish community and its members. In the previous pages I have tried to provide education and enlightenment about the problem of addiction and our lack of awareness. But once I have done so, I wish to better understand what holds us back from doing what is necessary to promote helpful and evidence-based treatments and recovery. What is the nature of our resistance? If our goal is, in the words of the Deuteronomist, is to "choose life," (Deuteronomy 30:19) why do we shut our eyes to life-threatening problems and resist treatments and methods that have been medically proven to

---

6   William R. Miller and Steven Rollick, *Motivational Interviewing: Preparing People for Change*, 2nd ed. (New York and London: The Guilford Press, 2002).

7   Ibid., p.22.

be successful? In the future, I hope to discover some answers to this perplexing problem, but I will only do so by listening to and learning from those who either disagree with me or those who simply refuse to seriously address the issue of addiction. This can only happen if our synagogues, Federations and JCCs are willing to engage in a conversation about addiction and recovery. Until then, we will remain inside a spiritual fog that will cause irreparable damage.

Moses went through two identifiable phases in the Precontemplation stage. During the first, he was growing up in Pharaoh's palace as a prince of Egypt, seemingly unaware of his enslaved people's suffering (though the Midrash addresses the question of whether and how he became aware of his Hebrew identity, the Torah text is not explicit about this). Then, in Exodus 2:11 we suddenly learn that Moses "went out to his kinsfolk and witnessed their labors." The great medieval commentator Rashi explains that this witnessing entailed a true identification with their pain and suffering. It is hard to imagine that had Moses already known his real identity, he could be so impervious to his people's travails. But this is what people in Precontemplation do. They are often unaware of their own pain or of what other people are going through. Moses reaches the Action stage very swiftly when he kills the Egyptian who is beating a Hebrew. He is now forced to flee Egypt.

The second Precontemplation stage spans a period (according to the Midrash) of almost 40 years when, having escaped Egypt, Moses marries Zipporah and settles in Midian. It is there that he raises a family and becomes a shepherd for his father Jethro. As far as we know, he becomes comfortable in Midian, in his new life. Does he ever think about his people back in Egypt? Does he still feel some measure of their agony? We don't know, and the Torah text provides little or no clue about Moses frame of mind during his years as a Midianite shepherd. So for the sake of argument, let's imagine that as he tends his father-in-law's flocks, cohabits with his wife and raises his two sons, the memories of his identification with the Israelites' suffering fades into history. The thought of returning to Egypt to rescue them is the furthest thing from his mind. So imagine his surprise, an unpleasant one for him indeed, when he encounters God at the burning bush and learns of God's intention to send him back to Egypt to lead his people out of slavery. The fog of Precontemplation has clouded his vision and feelings until this moment, when he is shaken out of complacency and summoned into a life of prophecy and leadership.

Like some of the later prophets such as Jeremiah and Jonah, Moses is resistant to God's call. The resistance is powerful. The last thing Moses wants to do is leave his comfy life for an iffy proposition. And like so many other precontemplatives, he seems unwilling to admit that a serious problem exists, one that involves others being harmed. God's role becomes especially informative here. In the dialogue at the burning bush in Exodus chapters 3-4, as God continues to explain the upcoming mission, Moses comes up with questions and/or objections five times. Only at the fifth, when Moses asks God to send someone else, does God become angry. Until that point, God patiently answered each objection and was empathetic with Moses' resistance. Even when God finally becomes exasperated, God still answers Moses objection by showing him the possibility of his brother Aaron acting as his spokesman.

Through God and because of God's ability to come alongside Moses in his resistance, Moses is able, by the end of the dialogue, to find the motivation and strength to initiate the mission and begin a new life as prophet, leader and lawgiver. Had God forced Moses earlier, or shut him down, or refused to empathize with Moses' reluctance to leave a comfortable life for a series of unknowns, the results could have been very different. At least two key lessons about the two main players emerge from this story. Moses shows the potential for personal growth and the faith to lead his people out of slavery into freedom. God emerges as a proficient counselor who can listen, empathize and motivate.

The spiritual fog will be lifted when those of us who suffer from addiction and the rest of us who are witnesses demonstrate a willingness to grow and change. Addicted people will progress through the Sages of Change into a readiness for positive action and healing. Their family and friends will cease judging, lecturing and cajoling them and give them the room to stand or fall on their own, while knowing all along that if they fall, they will not be alone. A loving and supportive community will be there to help, a community that can empathize with those suffering from the addiction disease. Such a community will not fall into the trap of moralism about a condition that people do not choose. The Jewish world will come alongside anyone with an addiction problem and say, "We may not be able to feel exactly what you are experiencing, but we will not judge you for it. We may not truly comprehend why you behave the way you do, and we may not condone destructive and harmful behaviors, but we will be there to listen, support and offer guidance and love." Like God patiently walking Moses through his resistance at the burning bush, the Jewish community will learn to see addiction for what it is and take positive steps to alleviate the terrible harm it can cause. And the ones afflicted with addiction will take heart and have the courage to change.

Part Two

LIFTING THE FOG

Chapter 1

THE "MIRACLE" OF RECOVERY?

How does change come about? Especially a shift so drastic that would move an addicted person into recovery or a family crazed with codependence into healthy detachment? The Stages of Change model, introduced for discussion in the last chapter, implies that change is a dynamic process. I believe we delude ourselves if we believe change typically happens suddenly, as if by magic or through some revelatory moment or epiphany alone. Some people fortunate enough to have found recovery claim to have had this kind of experience; Bill Wilson, the co-founder of Alcoholics Anonymous is a notable example, when he beheld that great flash of white light that he often spoke about later on.[1] (It is notable that he experienced this while in treatment in a sanitarium for alcoholism, placing the revelatory moment within a process of change and healing. More on this later.) I think Bill's epiphany, along with others like it, is more the exception than the norm. Most people will never see the light in that remarkable way. But they nevertheless will need treatment if they are to succeed in sustaining long-term recovery and reclaiming their spiritual and essential self.

As the addicted person or her family moves from the Contemplation stage into Preparation, dramatic shifts indeed do occur. It begins to dawn on her that the drawbacks of the addicted life are more significant than the benefits. The intoxicating effects of the drug are no longer as fun or exciting as they had been. The problems that ensue from heavy use can no longer be denied. As the brain develops increased tolerance for the drug, compulsions and physical and emotional cravings become overpowering. The family members have, most likely, already concluded that their loved one's use is a matter of concern. But now they are starting to realize that all their attempts to influence and change her have come to naught. As is often mentioned in 12 Step rooms, they are understanding that their pattern of repeating the same strategies over and over again while expecting

---

1   This event is described in Susan Cheever's biography of Bill Wilson, *My Name is Bill* (New York: Simon and Schuster, 2004), p. 118.

different results has become a kind of insanity.

Another popular statement often heard in the rooms is "I'm sick and tired of being sick and tired." Again, this is a sentiment shared both by the addicted person and her loved ones. Tectonic shifts are now happening deep within the foundation of the diseased human soul. The divine spark within, crying out for life, is being noticed and heeded. In the Preparation Stage, positive steps are initiated, and the Action Stage is just around the corner: for the addicted person, this usually means treatment. For the family members and loved ones this can mean therapy and/or Al Anon.

People in recovery often speak of the "miracle of recovery." This is a term heard frequently in 12 Step fellowships. I have no doubt that someone who has hit bottom and somehow finds sobriety can experience this as a miracle. In the Big Book of Alcoholics Anonymous, the final section ("They Lost Nearly All") consists of personal stories told by 15 alcoholics who were on the verge of total collapse, both physical, mental, emotional and spiritual.[2] These stories are framed as testimonies of the miraculous divine intervention that can rescue a dying alcoholic and, through a providential kind of grace, give him a new lease on life, a new beginning. One cannot help but be moved and inspired by these accounts.

And yet...

The language of miracles is not universally embraced, nor is it universally applicable. The Jewish Sages, followed by theologians and philosophers like Maimonides, had different opinions about the meaning of miracles. Some believed that miracles are divine interventions that defy the natural order. Others held that miracles are themselves part of the natural order. This view is reflected in chapter 5 of "Pirkei Avot" (Sayings of the Fathers): "Ten things were created on the eve of the Sabbath during twilight," and the list includes the rainbow (Genesis 9:12-17), the manna in the desert (Exodus 16), Balaam's talking ass (Numbers 22:21-35), the earth that opened up and swallowed Korah and his followers (Numbers 16:31-34). The Sages were suggesting that miracles are really part of the created order of the world, part of the Divine Plan, rather than amazing, nature-defying episodes. In other words, the potential for the miraculous is somehow built into the fabric of nature.

Understood in this light, recovery from addiction is usually a

---

2   *Alcoholics Anonymous,* 3rd ed., pp. 457-558.

process rooted in the person's biology, psychology and spirituality. It is miraculous in the sense that the person's ability to change seems to defy all odds. Reversing the juggernaut of compulsive drug use is a daunting prospect, but the shift occurs as part of a process of change. In this sense, recovery is more process than event, a deep internal turning towards health that comes from within the human soul rather than a miraculous intervention from the outside.

I have no argument with those who claim to have been saved by divine intervention or who talk about the recovery process as if it were a miraculous event. Their story is always an inspiring one. Those who hear it may be moved to make positive changes themselves.

However, this model doesn't apply to everyone who finds his way into recovery. The alchemy of miraculous intervention, otherwise known as a conversionary experience, may be something people pray, hope and wait for. It certainly has worked for many. But not for everyone. If a person is contemplating change and thinking about getting into recovery, and if she believes that a miracle is what is needed for her to embark on that path, she may never make the leap forward. Instead, she might fool herself into imagining that as long as God hasn't sent her a sign, she may as well keep drinking or using.

Recovery is a process, often a painfully slow one. It can take months, even years to reach the decision to make preparations and take actions to change. Recovery doesn't start once the addicted person stops or curtails his use. Rather, its genesis extends back to the moments when he begins contemplating the desirability of changing his drinking or drugging habits, when he begins to see the drawbacks of the addicted life. This process is biological, psychological and spiritual. Biological and psychological, because the brain sickness caused by the drug use triggers an emotional response akin to waking up from a nightmare or emerging from a dark tunnel. This may happen sporadically or frequently before the addicted person starts to make positive changes, and there is no common timeline or schedule. The spiritual side becomes stirred by the body's and brain's growing awareness of the promise of a better, healthier life. The person's soul is moved to begin climbing out of the dark pit and take its place in the sunlight of hope and recovery. This can happen like a flash or, more commonly, like a dawning realization, a series of steps along a path that can often seem like an obstacle course.

I wonder what Joseph was thinking about after his jealous brothers cast him into the pit, or what Jonah was thinking about while sitting in

The "Miracle" of Recovery?

the belly of the great fish for three days. Both biblical characters started out with a notable degree of self-centeredness. Were they completely and immediately transformed by these traumatic events? It took some time for Joseph to really grow up and for Jonah to grow out of his selfishness and primary concern for his own reputation as a prophet. Joseph quickly rose up to become head of Potiphar's household, but who knows how competitive and even ruthless he must have been to do so? As Pharaoh's grand vizier, were Joseph's actions always ethical and compassionate? And at the end of the Jonah story we see that he is still fretting about his reputation and his physical comfort.

Recovery happens slowly, healing can be a long, sometimes painful and frustrating journey. People change at their own pace, and vestiges of their old ways often linger. Later in Part Three I will discuss where slips and relapses fit in this recovery path, but in the present context I must emphasize that setbacks in the journey are signs and reminders that the recovery process is not magical, easy or instantaneous. Turning over a new leaf usually doesn't happen overnight.

The move into treatment and recovery can signify a new beginning, the beginning to re-establish positive connections, to rebuild positive relationships, to encounter others and the world in a new way in recovery. This is where the possibility of Buber's I-Thou model can emerge. For the person in recovery starts to see others as people in their own right, human beings who are not merely objects to meet his needs but subjects like himself, who have their own needs and feelings. As the fog of addiction is lifting, he is more able to put himself in other peoples' shoes and develop empathy. Once this happens, he can connect with them in a loving and spiritual way. The I-It world of experience still occupies most of his being as it does for us all. But the light of recovery allows the I-Thou world of love and interconnectedness to shine through.

Chapter 2

FROM PREPARATION TO ACTION

In general, the addicted individual needs to go through the Stages of Change in order, without skipping or artificially accelerating. For example, skipping the Contemplation stage and moving directly from Precontemplation to Preparation might result from some type of external coercion like incarceration or hospitalization. One moment he is actively using drugs and claims to see no problem with it (Precontemplation), the next moment he is suddenly looking for treatment options (Preparation). The change that is externally driven may be genuine and may have a permanent positive impact. However, the type of change that is internally driven usually has a more lasting effect.

The addicted person is coming to understand how deeply he has been hurting himself and others. He is starting to emerge from the shadow of his own exhaustive needs and is learning to empathize with those who have been affected by his addictive behaviors. Things are beginning to click for him in new and unexpected ways. He is moving beyond the Contemplation stage as he now plans to really do something about his problem. While contemplating the change, he was thinking, "I've really got to start getting serious about getting out of this addiction life, maybe in a few months or so." Now that he has moved into the Preparation stage he is thinking, "This has got to stop, and soon! Time for me to find a program, to get help." If he has the luxury of doing this on his own, without the external prompts of the criminal justice or Department of Children and Families (DCF) system or out of medical necessity, he is stirred by an internal process of emotional and spiritual growth that can have long lasting effects.

There are many notable exceptions. Some individuals fall back from a commitment to change to their old habits and ways, even after going through a process of internal positive growth. Others almost instantaneously get sober because someone is telling them to, and their change takes hold and becomes permanent. In the clinic where I worked, some of the patients articulated an artificial polarized culture by claiming they were in treatment out of choice while others were there because they "had to be." I would often remind them that no one was forced to be in treatment, that it was always a choice. The patient who opted for treatment instead of jail or losing custodial rights over her children was still making a conscious decision: better to get help than to sit in a cell or witness the removal of her children. I would frequently witness success stories when the person who was court or DCF-involved was able to truly benefit from all we had to offer. At the beginning she may have appeared resistant, sullen and angry but as the treatment episode progressed she showed signs that she was taking it all in and internalizing what she was learning. Her outcome, and those like her, could be a bright one. In cases like this, I would take great pleasure in writing a letter on her behalf to the judge or the DCF caseworker reporting her successful achievement of her Treatment Plan goals. I would always show the letters to my patients and I would observe their reaction as they heard or read the laudatory words confirming their success. Their sense of pride and self worth was clearly visible on their faces. Their expressions of gratitude to me were priceless.

"Fake it till you make it" is a slogan often cited in 12 Step fellowships. Newcomers are urged to go through the motions of recovery even if they haven't internalized the commitment to change. For example, people who haven't achieved full sobriety are still encouraged to attend 12 Step meetings. Perhaps some positive messages and lessons will start sinking in. In the clinic where I worked, patients were expected to participate in groups even when they were resistant, with the hope that they would begin to feel increased motivation for change. People can move from Preparation to Action even if they are "faking it."

The Rabbinic Sages taught: "*mi-tokh lo lishma ba lishma,* (Talmud Pesachim 50b)," literally translated as "[acts that are done] not for their own sake [can] lead to [acts done] for their own sake." The Sages were teaching an early version of "fake it till you make it." They were saying that it is common for an individual to perform a mitzvah perfunctorily, especially when first embarking on the religious journey. Prayer is a good example. Because prayer is a daily obligation, it is natural to recite the prayers in rote fashion. This is true even for experienced worshipers. The notion of *lo lishma* indicates not only a mechanical practice but also the expectation of some reward. The worshiper might be thinking that the act of prayer will bring some magical results like good health or prosperity. But the Sages would have exhorted him to keep praying regardless of the motivation with the hope that eventually he would be motivated by the wish to perform a mitzvah for its own sake, out of a sense of obligation or the satisfaction derived from performing the act, rather than out of a wish for compensation.

As the addicted person moves from Preparation into Action, the expectation of reward is completely natural, even healthy. When she stops drinking or using drugs, she expects her life to improve. Her executive functioning is now freed from the shackles of the drug of necessity, her brain and body are starting to heal, she now finds herself able to work, pay the bills, get along better with people around her. The fruits of her recovery efforts are becoming more evident. But what happens when, in spite of all these herculean efforts, she gets laid off from her job, or her husband decides to exit the marriage, or she develops a severe health condition? That is when the true test comes. Can she sustain her commitment to recovery in the wake of these dashed hopes? Can she justify her continued recovery work while admitting that life can still be harsh and while the rewards of a healthier life remain elusive?

If we accept the notion that recovery is usually an organic process, the inevitable setbacks will be overcome through motivation and clarity of will. This is not to imply that willpower is all that is needed to break the cycle of addiction. That would align with the Moral model of addiction. Yet if a person has moved through the Stages of Change organically, he will be more equipped to withstand the obstacles that threaten his progress. He has already shown signs of emotional, physical and spiritual healing. He has concluded that the addicted life is much more harmful than beneficial. His positive thinking and reflections on the hope for recovery allow him to naturally evolve into a path towards health. As this occurs, the brain and body are starting to heal and the thought process follows suit. Pitfalls are bound to turn up. They are not roadblocks; they are hurdles to overcome.

As discussed in the last chapter, I believe recovery "miracles" are less common than the natural journey of healing. The conversionary event eludes most people. However, in the minority of cases where a perceived divine intervention propels individuals into dramatic change, they may be less equipped to handle the obstacles to recovery. This could have something to do with how the miraculous event can shape their expectations and the way they relate to God's role in their healing. They might be thinking: "If God has brought this miracle to me, why is God making it so easy for me to want to give up? Why is

God testing me in this way?" The miracle path might be accompanied by the magical expectation that since their recovery is God's will, God ought to be engineering a smooth recovery path for them. Once the path becomes too shaky or difficult, the vestiges of addictive thinking creep back in. Now the thinking sounds like: "It's not worth all the effort, in spite of all I've been doing I'm still struggling, I might as well go back to using."

For the person who has organically moved from addiction into recovery, such thinking is less likely. The expectations are more realistic. The blinders are off. No one really imagines that the process should or will be easy. Instead, the one who travels this natural recovery path will already be developing the coping skills to handle the inevitable triggers and hurdles along the way.

Here's a case in point. One of our veteran patients, Joe M. was receiving outpatient treatment for severe cocaine use disorder. Our clinic's policy endorsed keeping people in treatment as long is they felt the benefit, regardless of insurance or the patient's ability to pay. Joe was in his 40s with a long history of incarceration. He attended groups regularly, tended to be quiet during the sessions and showed no signs of curtailing or stopping his cocaine use. Because the clinic utilized a team approach, I was one of several counselors who had direct contact with Joe. We would ask him to talk about his cocaine use. We would encourage him to be open about the benefits of the drug. Yet he was always reluctant to discuss his relationship with cocaine and he also tended to be very circumspect about other aspects of his life such as his living situation and ties with family and friends. So Joe continued to stay stuck in his pattern of cocaine use and secretive demeanor with staff and peers in the clinic.

Or so it seemed. One of the things Joe had kept from us was his dependence on opioids. But at a certain point he became upset enough about the opioid use and its effects that he decided to disclose this to a staff member. Joe had had some trouble with opioids in the past but he never had wanted to start methadone treatment. Meanwhile, our clinic had started to provide buprenorphine as an alternative approach to opioid use disorders and Joe heard about this. He was admitted to the MAT track in our program and was prescribed 24 mg per day of Suboxone (the sublingual formulation of buprenorphine plus Naloxone), the highest dose allowed by our MD. Joe would be required to meet individually with one of us every week in order to receive his prescriptions. He continued to be very closed off, reluctant to talk about himself and his issues. However, we noticed immediately that the Suboxone was enabling him to stop using illicit opioids (his UTOX results were consistently negative for opioids). That meant the treatment was working for him because he was experiencing the outcome he had hoped for when he started MAT with us. He was no longer using illicit opioids.

But the cocaine problem persisted. And the pattern was always the same. Joe would sit down with one of us, we would review his UTOX results and compliment him on the absence of illicit opioids. Then we would question him about the presence of cocaine in virtually every weekly sample. He never wanted to talk about his cocaine use other than to admit that it was habitual. Occasionally his name would come up in staff meetings as someone who seemed to be making little progress. We somehow overlooked the reality of Joe's obvious progress according to his Treatment Plan, namely, his wish to stop using illicit opioids.

This pattern dragged on for a few years. Then, suddenly, the UTOX results started showing negative for cocaine. I remember asking him about his leap into sobriety and how he was able to account for his ability to stop the cocaine use. Perhaps I was expecting a story of some type of revelatory moment for Joe; so I was quite surprised when he told me, "I just stopped doing it. That's about it. I had enough."

Joe was not verbally articulate. He was very guarded and defended, possibly due to years of incarceration. But he was able to communicate to me that his decision to get completely sober was the result of an organic process of healing and growth. First the opioids, then the cocaine. As simple as that. No conversion event, no miraculous intervention that he could describe. As his brain, body and spirit healed from the heroin dependence, he eventually grew ready to forego cocaine and all psychoactive drugs. The process was a natural one for him. He didn't need to explain it. In today's parlance, he didn't just talk the talk, he walked the walk.

When it comes to the leap from Preparation to Action, no one size fits all. I have found that, having asked so many people to describe how they came to this decision, the majority were able to provide a natural and logical explanation. Physical health, family concerns, the wish to avoid incarceration, career motivation, all these were common factors in the shift towards recovery. Occasionally someone like Joe would emerge, one who had difficulty articulating the reasons behind moving into sobriety, yet these reasons were most likely organic and natural, not mystical or miraculous.

In general, once the addicted person learns to get out of his own way, a path to recovery can be cleared. A similar process holds true for families. Once families learn to step aside and practice healthy detachment, the "problem" person can start to take positive steps on his own. But this can be delayed as long as the family members fail to recognize that they are the problem as well.

Chapter 3

GETTING OUT OF THE WAY

One of my counseling instructors at Gateway Community College, Wendy Davenson, would refer to "enabling" as "killing with kindness." That description has stuck with me ever since I first heard it about 13 years ago.

She was an excellent teacher, and the course subject was Families and Addiction Counseling. When the subject of enabling came up, she was adamant that the family members' wish to protect and take care of their addicted loved ones could often turn into a pattern of doing for them what they could very well do for themselves. Those of us who are parents are quite knowledgeable about this. How often did we take over their homework, or make excuses for them with teachers and coaches, or walk them through situations when our involvement wasn't needed. With regard to addicted persons, the enabling can be more tempting and hence, more dangerous.

A few examples of enabling: Cynthia has developed a severe drinking problem that has interfered with her home and work life. On at least a few occasions her husband Brian has called her boss in the morning to report that she would not be coming to work that day due to illness. Brian is enabling her because he is assuming Cynthia's responsibility to directly communicate with her boss, plus he is making it easier for her to hold on to her job while drinking alcoholically. He is putting himself in the way of the inevitable consequences of her addiction, thereby preventing her from fully realizing her problem and getting the help she needs. Since alcoholism and drug addiction are potentially lethal diseases, Brian may be seen as actually killing Cynthia with kindness.

Wanda is married to Steve, who has been drinking heavily for several years. One night while asleep she was awoken by a loud thump on the floor next to her bed. Her husband had fallen out of bed in a drunken stupor. Wanda got out of bed and, with considerable effort, lifted Steve back into the bed. All the next day she was bothered by a nagging backache. Several weeks later the same thing happened again. But having already attended a few Al Anon meetings where she learned about detachment, this time she just let him lie on the cold floor for the rest of the night. She felt a little bad about doing this and spoke to her Al Anon sponsor who told her about the concept of detachment with love. So the next time Steve wound up on the bedroom floor, Wanda walked over to him, left him on the floor but placed a blanket over him to keep him warm through the night. (This anecdote is a rewrite of a story I found in one of the Al Anon conference-approved literature volumes.[1])

Her attempt to hoist Steve back into bed, at the cost of her own physical health and comfort, is a prime example of enabling. Her act of leaving him on the floor while covering him in a blanket is an illustration of detachment with love.

Jewish families understand enabling very well. We are experts at enmeshment.[2] Detachment seems to run against the grain for us. Over the years, especially since I became involved in Al Anon, several friends and acquaintances have been incredulous over my wife and my refusal to step in and try to influence our children's lives. Detachment can be truly painful. Setting boundaries and learning how to say "no" are very difficult. It seems that codependence is built into the very nature of Jewish families. I am sure our culture is not alone in this, but we have a way of putting our unique Jewish stamp on the phenomenon. It's called interference.

Just think of our matriarch Rebecca listening outside Isaac's tent while the old man sends Esau off to hunt and prepare the venison stew he loves so much. Rebecca must step in and change the plan. Or think of Sarah's insistence on the expulsion of Hagar and Ishmael. Or Joseph's insistence on his father and brothers' emigration from Canaan to Egypt, foreshadowing the years of enslavement to come. These Biblical interventions may have been necessary in order to guarantee the enactment of God's covenant with Abraham. But people got hurt as a result. Ishmael and Esau were cut off from their families of origin. Jacob's family who settled in Goshen would eventually become enslaved by Pharaoh. Since Biblical times, Jewish family members have been over-involved with each other.

It is in the nature of Jewish family members to be so interconnected as to blur the lines of individuation. The codependence comes in when

---

1 *Courage to Change: One Day at a Time in Al-Anon II*, (Virginia Beach: Al-Anon Family Groups, 1992), p. 22.

2 See Kerry Olitsky, *Recovery from Codependence: A Jewish Twelve Step Guide to Healing Your Soul* (Woodstock, VT: Jewish Lights, 2011).

we are unable to separate our own sense of well being from that of our loved ones. I may imagine my life is going well and my emotional equilibrium healthy, but then I notice how off balance and upset I become when my loved one is struggling. I immediately forget how well I've been doing because of my enmeshment with him.

However, enabling has its up side. In the world of addiction and treatment, the word "enabling" is always used pejoratively. But enabling can also mean empowerment. For example, in a counseling setting, the patient invariably benefits from the counselor's ability to enable him to achieve self-efficacy. This often requires the counselor to give the patient room to make his own decisions and his own mistakes. Once the patient learns from his errors, he is able to achieve goals on his own. He is empowered to succeed without the excessive interference of professionals. The same holds true in families. Once family members can get out of the way and stop enabling the addicted person by trying to take over his life and do for him what he can do himself, they can enable and empower him to find recovery.

Ever since Virginia Satir and others[3] began teaching in the 1950s that the family is really an interdynamic system, family therapy has grown remarkably as a tool to help struggling families survive and thrive. I am not a family therapist but I have seen how the different theories and techniques in family systems therapy can work so beautifully. Two approaches have been especially useful for me in my pastoral work and I know they are helpful for families affected by addiction: the mobile model and the family roles model. The mobile model suggests the image of a mobile, with its figures dangling on separate wires attached to a common shaft (e.g. the device hanging from the side of a baby's crib). The mobile represents a family system. Whenever one item is touched and moves, the other items immediately move in reaction. In a family where one member is considered the "problematic" one (Satir would refer to this as the "Identified Patient" or IP), the other members continually move or function in reaction to whatever she does. In the case of a family where one person has an addiction problem, whatever she does provokes reactions from the other immediate family members. Thus, they would have difficulty understanding their own roles as distinct from the IP. It follows that they would naturally blame the IP for the family's dysfunction. "We'd be fine if she weren't an addict," is the kind of statement you would

---

3   G. W. Brock and C.P. Barnard, *Procedures in Marriage and Family Therapy* (Needham Heights, MA: Allyn and Bacon, 1999).

hear in this type of family system. It is typical, and typically Jewish.

Family roles theory assigns roles to each child in a multi-child family.[4] One child may play the Jester role, another the Hero, another the Lost Child, another the Scapegoat. The addicted person is commonly the Scapegoat. She performs a needed function in the family: As the "problem child" or "black sheep" she makes it easier for the parents and other children to avoid looking at their own part in contributing to the family troubles. As long as this pattern persists, the family system will most likely erode or remain stagnant. Everyone will keep blaming the IP so they don't have to examine their own behaviors and attitudes. It's much easier that way, at least in the short run. In the long run, everyone loses.

The fog of addiction and harmful codependence begin to lift when families are confronted with an awareness that each member has a role to play that contributes to the dysfunction. They begin to see that it is unfair to blame the Scapegoat, or addicted person, or IP for all the travails. This process can unfold in a variety of settings but it is most often stimulated in treatment and self-help situations.

I recall participating in a family weekend at a wilderness treatment center where one of the activities was an enactment of a variation of the mobile model. We were to imagine that a square space in the middle of the room was a raft. Each family member, including the addicted person, was asked to take his place on the raft. Whenever the addicted person moved in any way, the rest of us were supposed to move in reaction, in order to try to keep the raft afloat. I remember the activity as somewhat fun, a little absurd and amusing, especially when we watched other families take their places on the imaginary raft. The message rang load and clear: As the addicted person moved, everyone else kept scrambling around the raft to compensate for the movement. They were the ones doing most of the work. The "problem child" didn't have to do very much.

Whether through treatment episodes with family components or through self-help programs such as Al Anon, any insight or awareness gained by the affected family members helps move them into the direction of positive change. Many Jewish families resist a posture of non-interference. We have trouble standing by inertly while a loved one struggles. We want to jump in and rescue. Fear and anxiety

---

4   For a summary of family roles theory, see Peter Myers and Norman Salt, *Becoming an Addictions Counselor* (Sudbury, MA: Jones and Bartlett, 2000), pp. 242-6.

generate dark visions of imaginary disastrous outcomes. Our guilty conscience kicks in and we can't bear the guilt caused by inaction. So we take on the responsibility for someone else's behaviors, falsely thinking we have the power to change him.

In self-help circles, the Serenity Prayer is often used as a support for an attitude of non-interference or detachment. "God, grant me the serenity to accept the things I cannot change" is interpreted to be a plea for the peace of mind that comes from realizing that we cannot change other people. It is hard enough to change ourselves. Changing others is nigh impossible. Throughout the years, I have referred many congregants and friends to Al Anon when they asked me what they should do about their loved one's drug or alcohol problem. Each time, I would ask them to check in with me at some point to let me know how it was going. I don't recall anyone following up with me. Does that mean they went to a meeting or two and then gave up, or perhaps they never went at all? I will never know. But I assume that in most cases, the Al Anon path was not taken, regardless of my advice. Is this because of a resistance to trying something new and foreign, or discomfort walking into a church and meeting strangers, or a fear of running into a friend or acquaintance, or an objection to the idea of detachment, or something else? I will never know this either, but I suppose all or some of these considerations apply.

Many of us fear a void. Empty space can be threatening. Moments of silence can feel like an eternity, so we rush in with speech. Inaction can feel dangerous. "Don't just sit there, do something!" is the rule. "Don't just do something, sit there!" seems wrong. But a posture of inaction is what is often called for when it comes to a loved one's addiction. And that is very hard for many Jews to swallow.

In the next chapter I will discuss types of interventions. There are certainly times when interventions are desirable, even necessary. In a life-threatening situation, drastic measures must be taken. In most cases, the slow burning process of addiction gives family members the room to carefully consider the best response. When active interventions are the rule, short-term outcomes may be positive, yet in the long run the addicted person could revert to previous patterns of use and manipulative behaviors. In the family system, if the members who are affected by someone's addiction are able to pause and begin taking a look at themselves while giving him the space to stumble, fall and rise up on his own, the long-term outcomes become more promising. The addicted person has been allowed the room to find self-efficacy, the family system has stepped aside to empower him to find his own way. The road may initially be quite bumpy, but in time the path will become smoother as he navigates his own recovery journey while his loved ones learn to live their own lives. No longer will they shoulder the burden of his struggles or allow their well-being to be determined by his. As they toil separately in the work of learning to find health and contentment on their own, eventually their paths will converge as they discover ways to inspire one another in their new consciousness.

If you are reading this and are looking for help, I offer the following recommendations:

- The National Institute for Drug Abuse (NIDA) is an excellent resource for educating oneself about addiction and mental health issues. Simply visit their website (www.drugabuse.gov) and click on the applicable links to read the most up to date and informative material about addiction.

- For more practical purposes, I highly recommend the SAMHSA website (Substance Abuse and Mental Health Services Administration), www.samhsa.gov. There you will find a hotline phone number (800-662-HELP), a treatment locator and downloadable pamphlets that will be useful. Two especially valuable readings for families affected by addiction are "What is Substance Abuse Treatment? A Booklet for Families" and "Family Therapy Can Help: For People in Recovery from Mental Illness or Addiction." These excellent pamphlets are free and easy to read. They also provide lists of additional resources at the end.

- Not every family visited by addiction needs treatment. Many families are able to develop healthy coping skills on their own, through their friends or with faith-based or self-help supports. But others may realize that their level of dysfunction requires professional intervention with a trained family therapist. If you are seeking options for family therapy, visit the website for the American Association for Marriage and Family Therapy (www.aamft.org) where you will find consumer information as well as a provider list. Then see which therapists will be covered by your medical insurance plan.

- Finally, if you are interested in self-help groups (more about the difference between self-help and treatment in the next chapter) visit the Al-Anon website (www.al-anon.org) or Nar-Anon (www.nar-anon.org). You will learn about how these peer support groups integrate a 12 Step approach with family specific issues and concerns. You will also be provided with links to find meetings in your area. Al-Anon has far more meetings than Nar-Anon. Though Al-Anon presents itself as a self-help group for families of alcoholics, it welcomes all families effected by chemical dependence.

Chapter 4

INTERVENTION, TREATMENT AND SELF-HELP

Let's start with some definitions of terms. Before we look at when interventions are necessary, it is important to discuss the word's meaning. Medically speaking, interventions are actions taken to interfere with or stop the progression of a disease. They are usually performed by medically trained professionals. In the world of addiction, intervention has become associated with drastic steps taken by family and friends, often with the help of a professional interventionist, to cajole the addicted person into accepting treatment. The term "intervention" also refers to the strategies, techniques and treatment modalities that are utilized to help an individual make progress in treatment. These actions are more effective when they are evidence-based and employed by credentialed counselors or therapists.

In popular culture today, partly due to the popularity of a television program called "Intervention," people have an image of a troubled individual who is unknowingly lured into a room populated by concerned friends and family and a trained intervention professional. She is essentially trapped and forced to hear statements by the participants, decrying her life style and addictive behaviors, revealing the deleterious effects of these behaviors on her loved ones. By appealing to her healthy side and her emotional attachment to her loved ones, they try to coerce her into agreeing to get immediate help.

The help that is proffered is some type of treatment, usually inpatient or residential. Here, the territory becomes especially murky and confusing. Addiction treatment has become an industry, a largely uncontrolled juggernaut where, without proper guidance and navigation, an individual can be subject to significant harm. When treatment is controlled and supervised by an authoritative licensing body, it can do much good. In such an instance, the treatment program is staffed by credentialed professionals who have earned licensure or certification in the addiction and mental health fields. The patient receives an initial intake and evaluation to assess her appropriateness for treatment. Together with a counselor or therapist she creates a Treatment Plan that is tailor-made specifically for her needs and goals. Based on the Treatment Plan, a strategy is devised that will address her place on the addiction and treatment spectrum. She will most likely participate in group and individual therapy, detailed progress notes will be recorded that will track her rehabilitation, her Treatment Plan will be periodically updated and a termination plan will be discussed almost from the beginning.

This can all take place either in a residential or outpatient setting, but the key considerations for "kosher" treatment are oversight and professionalism. Too many residential programs that profess to successfully rehabilitate addicted people fly under the radar of oversight by the state's department of health. Their staff members may not have the necessary credentials to pass muster as legitimate mental health providers. It is not sufficient for a staff member to claim legitimacy solely based upon her own history of addiction and recovery. It is also inappropriate for a staff person to claim legitimacy because she is a member of a 12 Step fellowship. Valuable as these types of experience may be, they do not equal education, training and thousands of hours of clinically supervised work, all of which are requirements for credentials.

12 Step programs like AA and NA are peer support or self help programs, distinct from treatment. They are not professionally driven. Every program member is considered equal, regardless of length of time in the fellowship or length of sobriety. Meetings are never facilitated by titled professionals who lend expertise to help others achieve and maintain stability in recovery. People draw experience, strength and hope from one another rather than from a counselor or clinician.

Family interventions may be intended to coax the addicted person into treatment or self help or both. When are they necessary? The Jewish values of *pikuah nefesh* (saving a life) and "Don't stand idly by the blood of your neighbor" (Leviticus 19:16) help inform the decision to take drastic measures. As discussed in the last chapter, enabling is doing for someone what they can do for themselves. Intervening is not necessarily enabling. According to my former clinical supervisor Peggy Whelan, who has been professionally involved in planned interventions, interventions are not meant to prevent the addicted person from experiencing the consequences of his use; rather, the intervention confronts him with *accountability* for the way his actions have affected his loved ones.

In addition, the Al-Anon value of minding one's own business and refraining from trying to step in to change others may be put aside when a person's life may be at stake. Understanding that addiction is a chronic, progressive and life-threatening disease, one may argue that intervention is always necessary because the subject's life is at stake as long as he's using. But there may not be an immediate threat. Interventions may be called for when the threat seems more at hand.

Teenagers appear to be most vulnerable to the ravages of addiction. Their adolescent brains have not yet reached maturity and addiction may stall their brain growth.[1] Plus, because they are usually more prone to taking risks, they venture into dangerous situations that would alarm their adults. Suburban teens go to the city to procure drugs, often to neighborhoods that are highly unsafe. They associate with people whose drug connections expose them to violence and crime. Finally, because their brains are still young, they may be prone to developing an addiction more quickly than adults.

Does this mean that teens heading toward, or already in the midst of addiction are always candidates for interventions? No. According to Ms. Whelan and many experts, it is usually wise to start with less drastic interventions such as getting them to meet with a school or private drug counselor or arranging an evaluation for treatment in an outpatient clinic. If they are using opioids, giving them and their adult family members a Narcan kit[2] is always warranted. Residential treatment is only relevant when other means of care and treatment have been exhausted.

Because so many Jewish parents are highly activist (some would say intrusive) with their children, they may be inclined to jump the gun and move directly into drastic interventions. Teenagers are usually rebellious by nature and attitude. They would probably be highly resistant to inpatient treatment, and the likelihood of a positive long (and even short) term outcome is reduced. Once they have moved through lower levels of care (like professional counseling

---

1   The adolescent brain generally does not reach maturity until age 25. See Arain, Mariam et al. "Maturation of the adolescent brain" *Neuropsychiatric Disease and Treatment* vol. 9 (2013): 449-61.

2   Narcan is the brand name for the opioid blocker Naloxone. It is administered either as an intramuscular injection or a nasal spray. The Naloxone immediately binds to the brain's opioid receptors and reverses the effects of the opioids that are causing overdose.

and outpatient services), their parents and loved ones can insist that something more is needed because nothing has worked until now.

When a parent of children, especially small children, is abusing drugs or alcohol, a drastic intervention may be necessary. Unlike the teenager, the addicted parent is more likely to have an awareness that his drug use is problematic, especially in light of its impact on his ability to fulfill parental responsibilities. Even so, he still may be in the Precontemplative or Contemplative Stage of Change, unwilling to move directly into treatment. As the children continue to be impacted, whether through neglect or outright abuse, the adult relatives realize that it is too risky to wait until the addicted father takes his own initiative. The time for action is now, and an intervention may be appropriate.

Typically, the "classic" intervention includes as many immediate family members as possible, along with closest friends. The goal is to show the addicted person that he is accountable for how his actions have hurt his loved ones and that there is an immediate remedy at hand. A professional who has experience in addictions counseling and in facilitating interventions is engaged. She may ask the loved ones to write letters to be read during the intervention. Preferably, she will collect the letters in advance and edit them for content. Accusatory and judgmental language should be avoided. The letters ought to consist of facts and events that clearly illustrate the addicted person's harmful behaviors and their effects on others. The letters should also contain emotional reactions such as hurt, confusion, disappointment, fear and alarm.

The family members have already worked out a plan with the professional so that all the participants are assembled and ready to receive the person in need of help. He is kept in the room as long as possible while the loved ones read their letters and share their concerns. Meanwhile, treatment options have already been investigated. The professional, with the family's input, has chosen one or two treatment programs with available beds so that an immediate transition can be made. Alternatively, an intensive outpatient program may be appropriate and the program has by now been selected. The financial and insurance arrangements (if applicable) have already been determined. The patient-to-be is reassured that his home and work obligations will be covered. In most cases, employers are required by law to provide leave (usually unpaid) for illness. The addicted person is reminded that, left unchecked, his addiction would probably lead to job termination anyway, or at least significant impairment in job performance.

The intervention may or may not result in treatment. But every intervention is successful in that the seeds have been planted, a learning process has begun that will most likely benefit the addicted person. The family members have taken the opportunity to express their concerns, fears and their love. And they will know that they have done everything in their power to help.

For tips and guidelines on interventions, visit the website of the National Council on Alcoholism and Drug Dependence (www.ncadd.org).

Chapter 5

THE WIDE WIDE WORLD OF TREATMENT

The thick fog of Precontemplation has lifted and the thinner fog of Contemplation has abated. The individual and/or her family are now taking steps in the Preparation stage to research options for treatment.

In the previous chapter I briefly discussed the difference between treatment and self help. As a reminder: self help is often a useful adjunct to treatment. But when the individual is in the acute phase of addiction, self help alone may not suffice. Many people don't seem to grasp this. They think AA alone is enough to support sobriety and recovery. For some people it is. For many it is not.

I can't fault those addicted persons and their families who shy away from the treatment route. It can be daunting at best and impossible at worst. There are so many options. Given that most people do not take the intervention path described in Chapter 4, where the professional helps direct the family towards the best treatment choice, the majority are left to their own devices. Word of mouth, the internet and advice from a trained addictions counselor are the most common vehicles of discovery. They can be as good or as bad as the sources consulted.

For instance, google the term "addiction treatment" and you will find pages and pages of websites that promote a wide variety of programs. It's enough to make one's head spin. Word of mouth may be unreliable when the testimonies are so individualized as to be irrelevant to the person now seeking help. Finally, the advice provided by the addictions counselor may not be based upon thorough research and investigation on her part, and if she doesn't really know the person needing treatment, her assessment may be skewed.

My intention in this chapter is to suggest some guidelines and considerations for those seeking treatment. It is not my purpose to recommend one treatment center over another or to provide definitive answers. Hopefully, after you read the following pages, you will have a better grasp of how to approach the difficult task of finding a program and what to avoid during the process.

Since this book is directed towards the Jewish community, let's start with the basic question: Should I or my loved one choose a Jewish treatment program? They do exist, on the east and west coast and even in more remote areas of the American heartland. In the heavily Jewishly populated regions such as New York and southern California, it is possible to find Jewish centers that offer outpatient as well as inpatient services. My purpose is not to catalog and rate them; rather, I am interested in exploring when and whether they are necessary or helpful at all.

As already stated, the myth "Jews Don't Use" has long been debunked. Yet the Jewish community has been slow in responding to the crisis of addiction and, in particular, the opioid epidemic. To the credit of certain insightful individuals, treatment programs with a Judaic orientation began to emerge about three decades ago. Most, if not all programs combine a faith-based Torah orientation with a Jewishly framed 12 Step approach. Some are affiliated with a particular denomination of American Judaism (Israel has a variety of programs that are religious and secular). The benefits of such programs are mostly anecdotal and difficult to qualify. One must rely almost entirely on reports and evaluations of ex-patients and the information is therefore subjective. Even so, I commend those who initiated and run these programs and I appreciate their willingness to confront head-on the problem of addiction among Jews.

Some addicted Jews are attracted to Jewish treatment programs for cultural or religious reasons. They may feel more comfortable around other Jews, or they may need a place that provides kosher food, Jewish worship and study. These reasons alone justify the value of specifically Jewish programs. Where else will a person be able to eat and pray according to her religious preferences while undergoing life changing therapy?

However, it is my impression that such people are a distinct minority. Most addicted Jews do not need Jewish oriented treatment. In fact, if they are dependent on opioids, they may not benefit from any Jewish program that would withhold Medication Assisted Treatment like methadone or buprenorphine. Jewish treatment centers that present Torah, worship, study and Jewish living as a panacea for recovery without allowing people the medication they need may be unintentionally causing harm. If opioid therapies like methadone are withheld from people with severe opioid use disorders, no amount of Torah study or prayer can adequately take the place of a medication that activates opioid brain receptors and prevents cravings and withdrawal symptoms. Without that medication, many (not all)[1] opioid dependent people will have trouble stabilizing and will remain at high risk for relapse, overdose and possible death.

If you are looking for a Jewish treatment program for yourself or a loved one and opioid dependence is involved, ask whether the program will provide transportation to either a methadone clinic or a buprenorphine provider. Find out whether the program would allow the take-home medication to be administered by a staff member. To my knowledge, many Jewish treatment programs disallow MAT for their patients. If this is the case, Jewish residential treatment should be a rule-out for most with opioid use disorders on the moderate or severe spectrum. Those with other addiction disorders and who are open to a faith-based approach may benefit from Jewish programs.

The above discussion may be a moot point if financial limitations exist. Notwithstanding the value of Jewish treatment centers, certain factors must come into play when investigating options for treatment. Insurance companies will not reimburse certain kinds of treatment in certain kinds of environments. They require a "failed" attempt in a lower level of care like general outpatient services before approving a higher level of care such as intensive outpatient or residential. Insurance companies will usually decline to help pay for treatment in facilities that do not offer a medical or evidence-based approach for their patients or who do not pass muster with their state health departments.

But I am getting ahead of myself. Let's assume that the addicted person and/or her family is in crisis. They are in the Preparation stage of change, ready to move into the Action stage once a program has been located. She (or they) have decided that finding a specifically Jewish program is not a priority. What should they do?

There is a common misconception that anyone with a serious chemical dependence problem needs to go directly to inpatient rehab in order to get well. The reason for this, at least in part, is the desperation factor: Family members are at the end of their rope, or the addicted person is desperate for immediate help and quick results. They believe that only a total immersion treatment experience will

---

1   The most recent edition of the Diagnostic and Statistical Manual of Mental Disorders (5th edition) distinguishes between mild, moderate and severe opioid use disorders. In milder cases of the disorder, Medication Assisted Treatment is less frequently called for.

do the trick, and that would entail at least a month in a residential facility. As previously mentioned, many people cannot afford this if they have to pay out of pocket. Plus, taking drastic measures is often unnecessary and does not guarantee a positive outcome.

In many places throughout the US and Canada one may dial 2-1-1 or visit www.211.org for free mental health resources and supports. The 2-1-1 systems are often connected with InfoLine and/or the United Way. They are staffed by trained phone personnel who are familiar with the resources available for people in need. It is also a good idea to check the treatment locator link in www.samhsa.gov. While you are doing all this, bear in mind that residential care is not the only effective treatment out there. Either you or your loved one may benefit from a low-pressure, less demanding outpatient program, especially if this is your first treatment event or if there is an unwillingness to leave home or work.

Visit the website for the American Society of Addiction Medicine (www.asam.org) to learn about their criteria for treatment and what is known as "Continuum of Care." This information is very useful for people who are starting to explore the arcane world of addiction treatment.

ASAM's Criteria and Continuum of Care have become standard and widely adopted guidelines for treatment providers, state Medicaid and insurance companies. All treatment planning and placement depend upon ASAM's Six Dimensions of Multi-Dimensional Assessment, to be determined through the cooperation of the patient and a clinical professional. The Dimensions are: Acute Intoxication and/or Withdrawal Potential; Biomedical Conditions and Complications; Emotional, Behavioral or Cognitive Conditions and Complications; Readiness to Change; Relapse, Continued Use or Continued Problem Potential; Recovery/Living Environment. The clinician learns about the presenting problems and seriousness of the patient's mental health condition in the Evaluation interview and considers all Six Dimensions before making any clinical recommendations.

The Continuum of Care is a numbered scale ranging from 1 (Outpatient services-OP) to 2 (Intensive Outpatient-IOP, Partial Hospitalization-PHP) to 3 (Residential/Inpatient-IP) to 4 (Medically Managed Inpatient services). Each level is subdivided into more specific varieties of treatment. For example, 2.1 refers to Intensive Outpatient, usually requiring a minimum of nine hours of treatment per week, three hours per day. 2.5 refers to Partial Hospitalization, a more intensive program than IOP where the patient may be expected to attend 5 days per week for 5 or 6 hours per day. These levels are used by the treatment providers and reimbursers (e.g. Medicaid or insurance companies) for billing and reimbursement purposes. The intensity of the level of care must match the clinical assessment of the patient's diagnosis and previous treatment experience. In other words, a person with no history of treatment would be placed in an OP or IOP level of care. If that turns out to be insufficient, she would move to a higher level of care.

Now let's return to the initialization of the Action Stage of Change. You have now chosen a program. Upon arrival to the clinic you or your loved one will receive an initial Intake and Screening. This is the preliminary entrance test, consisting of basic questions to determine whether you may be appropriate to be a patient in that facility. If you pass the Screening, you will most likely sit down with a credentialed professional for an Evaluation or Assessment. This process is much more in-depth than the initial Screening. The clinician will take a bio-psycho-social assessment in order to help you devise a Treatment Plan, the strategy that will guide your treatment experience. The Treatment Plan is based on the information you share and the clinician's assessment of your needs according to the Six Dimensions described above. In the plan, you will choose your treatment goals. Each goal will be sectioned into interventions and objectives. Together with the clinician, you will outline the steps you need to achieve your goals plus the strategies that will help you progress. The primary goals are directed towards the drug of choice and whether you are aiming towards total abstinence of decreased use. Other primary goals can be mental health-related issues such as depression or PTSD if applicable. Secondary goals can relate to problems such as unemployment, homelessness, relationship issues etc.

When the Evaluation is over, you will have an action plan with concrete goals, strategies and, hopefully, some kind of end plan or termination of treatment goal. If the clinician has been skillful you will feel hopeful and motivated to change. You have helped create your own coarse of treatment and you have agreed to give it your best effort. You are also placed in a level of treatment that fits you best. You will be able to fit the demands of the program into your schedule. You will also not go broke from this treatment episode because either insurance or state Medicaid is helping to foot the bill. Perhaps you will receive some financial support from family members or you may

The Wide Wide World of Treatment

need to dip into your savings if you have any left. The bottom line: you have been thrown a lifeline and you are eager to grasp it.

If this is a first or second attempt at treatment, you may do very well following the treatment guidelines while remaining at home and going to work if you have a job. Don't automatically assume you have to go away for months at a time in order to get better. More research is emerging that supports treatment while living at home and learning to apply recovery principles and lessons to life in one's own familiar environment, often combined with a 12 Step program. It may feel easier or more promising to achieve and maintain sobriety in a far away place, removed from the risks and harmful influences of the home, neighborhood or workplace. But eventually the inpatient program ends. You might transition to a halfway house for a while. But unless you decide to relocate altogether, you will wind up back home, surrounded by many of the old triggers and influences. An OP, IOP or PHP can give you the tools for successful recovery without giving up your familiar environment, if possible.

The world of residential treatment is replete with programs that boast successful outcomes. Many inpatient centers are run by highly skilled and well-trained professionals. Others are staffed by people who believe they are qualified to provide expert help because they themselves were once addicted and are now in recovery. Some programs are, in effect, scam operations that claim to have the best cure and the best results. These places tend to be wildly expensive. They may report very high percentages of "graduates" who have remained clean and sober after an extended period. I am automatically suspicious of any program that makes such claims. How do they collect their data? How can they really know if an ex-patient has not relapsed? Some of these places conduct phone surveys several months after completion of treatment and ask the respondents if they have relapsed. When the answer is no, how is one to know whether the ex-patients are being entirely truthful? Perhaps they are ashamed to admit failure so they tell the questioner what they think he wants to hear. It is very difficult to collect reliable data from graduates of IP programs unless they are on sight and re-evaluated by a clinical professional.

Beware of scams and places that claim to have all the answers. Addiction Treatment is highly specialized and extraordinarily complex. Experimental models masquerading as evidence-based or medically proven systems are to be avoided. If you are considering a particular program, ask for their credentials. Who provides their oversight? Are they accredited by their state's department of health or CARF (Commission on Accreditation of Rehabilitation Facilities)? Do they use evidence-based modalities and treatment techniques such as cognitive or dialectical behavioral therapy or motivational enhancement therapy? If they are faith based programs do they also follow a medical model of treatment?

The wide, wide world of treatment is confusing. Just dipping into the deep waters of that turbulent ocean can make one want to stay on dry land. But if an individual or family approaches the task of investigating treatment options with eyes wide open and with the right questions, the process need not be so forbidding. Sometimes the right direction is more obvious than meets the eye. Sometimes the best option becomes clear and readily available. And it is also comforting to know that if the first try doesn't "work," many other alternatives still exist. Keeping this in mind can help family members maintain a clear perspective while the treatment episode is in progress.

Chapter 6

THE VIEW FROM THE GRANDSTAND

The addicted individual is finally in treatment. Her loved ones are breathing a collective sigh of relief. They might be silently reciting the *Shehechiyanu* blessing ("Praised are You, Lord our God, Sovereign of the universe, who has kept us in life, sustained us and enabled us to reach this day!"). Her loved ones are most likely feeling hopeful. Whether this is a first-time treatment or not, close family members and friends are praying that this episode will do the trick. It is as if they are sitting in the grandstand cheering for their favorite sports team.

But those sports fans also know how powerless they are. Not over themselves, but over the outcome. They may yell and cheer as loud as they can, they may pray as hard as they can, but their efforts have no bearing on whether their chosen team will win or lose. I have attended many sports events in my life and I often wonder at the emotional intensity of the fans. I have been a New York Mets and Duke (my alma mater) basketball fan for years; I love it when my teams win and I am disappointed when they lose (alas, a common pattern for my Mets). Even when I am watching the games on TV, I find myself yelling at the players, cheering when they make great plays, groaning when they fail. Yet I have no illusion that my involvement has any bearing on the outcome of the game.

The sports analogy is apt for loved ones of addicted people currently in treatment. Family and friends are rooting for them, cheering them on from the grandstand. At the same time, they would do well to keep an attitude of healthy detachment. The patient in treatment is traveling on her own recovery path. Family and friends are not responsible for her ongoing sobriety. They are only responsible for maintaining a clear and positive perspective.

Here are a few tips for family and friends of addicted individuals receiving treatment. These tips also apply to the time when treatment is not occurring, but they may be especially helpful during a treatment episode, when loved ones can create some space to do their own internal work and fortify themselves for the day when the treatment has concluded.

1. Consider attending Al-Anon meetings.

As mentioned earlier, Al-Anon is a 12 Step program for families and friends of people with alcoholism. Other addictions are also welcome. The program was created by Lois Wilson (the wife of Bill Wilson, co-founder of AA) and her friends in 1952 and is based upon the same 12 Steps of AA. Many Jews shun Al-Anon because they are reluctant to give up the illusion of control, and they may be uncomfortable with the fact that the meeting is held in a church and could end with the Lord's Prayer. But the program can be immensely helpful as a peer support network where one can learn the value of detachment and the need to shift the focus away from the addicted person and onto the loved one who is affected by the addiction. If you attend your first meeting as a newcomer you will be encouraged to go to at least six meetings to see if the program can work for you. This is reasonable because you may be shell-shocked during the first few meetings but you might start coming to your senses as you continue to attend.

Visit the Ala-Anon website at www.al-anon.org to read about the program and to locate a meeting near you.

2. Don't count on this treatment episode to do the trick.

I believe treatment works. But it isn't simply a matter of success or failure. A "successful" treatment episode doesn't necessarily amount to long-term or permanent sobriety. A person may complete a program and benefit from what he has learned even if he eventually relapses. Each treatment experience plants new seeds in the garden of recovery. The seeds can bear fruit immediately or over the course of months or years.

I have often heard professionals and lay people say relapse is part of recovery. They are trying to point out that relapsing can be part of the recovery journey. If someone relapses, it doesn't necessarily mean he has to start over. He has already made progress in his recovery before the relapse. But I have a problem with "relapse is part of recovery": It can imply that relapsing is an acceptable if not positive step along the recovery journey. This is not a message that ought to be conveyed. Relapse can be dangerous, even fatal. It is not OK.

As mentioned earlier, I view relapse not as part of recovery but as a symptom of the addiction disease. As a symptom, it needs to be taken seriously and it is often a cue that further treatment is necessary.

Over the years I have observed many people, especially parents and spouses of addicted individuals, who express a blend of relief and intense anxiety while their loved ones are undergoing treatment. They pray that the treatment will bring about a "cure," or at least a sustained period of recovery. They can conjure fantasy stories about the end of the drug-using nightmare and the beginning of a productive, sober life. This is completely normal and to be expected. However, it is important to separate the fantasy and dreams from the reality based upon experience. It is most likely that their loved one will pick up drugs or alcohol again at some point. It could either be a slip – a one time brief setback or a full blown relapse, involving days, weeks, months or years of sustained drug use. Family and friends would do well to remember that a slip or relapse doesn't constitute absolute failure, nor does it indicate a flaw in the type of treatment of program that preceded it. Ironically, loved ones can find comfort knowing that the journey of treatment and recovery is a long one; when slips or releases occur, many more chances for successful treatment emerge. Eventually, long-term, sustained recovery may prevail.

3. Take good care of yourself.

Self care is always a good idea in any circumstance. It is a true necessity while one is in the midst of a stressful situation. Years ago when my wife and I were dealing with an addiction crisis in our family, I became so enmeshed in our troubles that I lost almost all sense of boundaries between us and our loved one. I had trouble sleeping and I neglected my health. As a result I had a severe flare-up of Crohn's Disease resulting in hospitalization, after 30 years of remission. I learned my lesson the hard way. I eventually came to embrace the need for good self care, including sleep, exercise, diet, rest, fun and leisure, prayer and meditation.

It may be hard to give yourself permission to focus on your own physical, emotional and spiritual health while knowing that your loved one is struggling. This holds true whether he is in or out of treatment, whether he is living within your orbit or outside of it. As I discussed in Part One, codependence comes naturally for us Jews. We wear the codependence *kippah* (skullcap) quite naturally. So it requires significant effort to put aside the troubles of our addicted loved one and focus on ourselves.

If he is away in a residential program, the ability to focus on self-care is much easier. You are not seeing him regularly and you are placing your hopes and trust in the program's ability to help him find and sustain recovery. You are acutely aware that the clock is ticking and he will eventually complete the program. Therefore, the best time to shift gears and take care of yourself is while he is away. In so doing, you are fortifying yourself for the after-treatment phase. And if you develop a solid regimen of self-care, you will have a better chance to maintain it later on. Not only will you be the beneficiary, but he will too. There is nothing he would like more, after he completes treatment, than having you off his back.

4. Consider attending synagogue.
If you are already a member of a synagogue, think about increasing your attendance at worship and study sessions. If you are not yet a member anywhere, go out and do some "shul shopping." This tip is obviously not for everyone, but even secular-minded Jews can find rewards in synagogue involvement. Be sure you are affiliated with a congregation where the rabbi is available and open-minded. Taking the time to pray and study *in a community* is like giving yourself a well deserved gift.

Being a family member of an addicted individual is immensely isolating. The shame and embarrassment, especially for Jewish families, are palpable. That is why Al-Anon is such a good idea. It provides fellowship and the constant reminder that you are not alone. Synagogues ought to be able to provide another comforting social outlet for all Jews who are hurting and in need of spiritual solace. The more you can emerge from your social isolation chamber, the better your own adjustment to life with an addicted person will be – especially once she finishes her treatment episode.

5. Gradually and carefully start to share your story with others.
I use both words "gradually" and "carefully" to remind you of two basic truths: **One**, revealing the story all at once to many people whom you know can expose you to vulnerability and a flood of well-meaning so-called experts who really don't know very much about addiction and recovery. It is far better to choose a few people with whom you are close. If you've been hiding your plight from them until now, muster the courage to disclose the situation. Now that your loved one is finally getting help, it is time for you too to get support

from your closest friends. Let yourself out of your isolation and shame by including a few others in your story. As it is often said in 12 Step rooms, we are only as sick as our secrets.

Two: choose carefully whom you wish to share with. This person should be accepting, tolerant and non-judgmental. He may be family or a friend of an addicted individual. Or she may be in recovery from addiction herself. Neither is a guarantee that this is the best person to take into your confidence. I have known many people affected by chemical dependence who were judgmental and who believed that their own recovery path was the only right one. Therefore, direct experience with addiction is not a prerequisite. A non-judgmental attitude is.

6. Take some time to educate yourself about other treatment programs and options.

Chemical dependence is a chronic, relapsing condition. As much as you hope the current treatment episode will put your loved one on the road to permanent recovery, chances of recidivism are significant.

If you look up Stages of Change on the internet, you will find reference to *six* stages rather than five. Many sources label the sixth stage "Termination," signifying a cure and end of the problematic condition. Other sources label the sixth stage "Relapse,"[1] obviously a far cry from Termination. Prochaska and DiClemente may originally have suggested Termination as a sixth stage, but many more people end up relapsing. With this in mind, it is always a good idea to do some research about other treatment options even while your loved one is undergoing treatment. He may exit the program before completion or relapse shortly thereafter. You will want to have your ducks in a row should you need to guide him in a different direction.

As mentioned earlier, inpatient programs can be prohibitively expensive if they are not state-run or heavily subsidized. Outpatient programs can be quite effective in providing tools for recovery and relapse prevention while helping one to remain in one's community. A myriad of treatment choices can be found in the SAMHSA treatment locator link on the agency's website. Do some reading, make a few

---

1 For an example, see https://www.verywellmind.com/the-stages-of-change-2794868. Prochaska has insisted that he never intended Relapse to be considered a Stage of Change (Prochaska and Velicer, *The Transtheoretical model of Health Behavior change*, [American Journal of Health Promotion 1997;1211]:38-48.).

phone calls to potential providers. Don't make this a full time project. Keep the self-care goals always in mind.

7. Take some time to educate yourself about the disease of addiction.

Addiction is hard to comprehend. Fortunately, many of us have had no need to educate ourselves about the cause and nature of chemical dependence. Whatever we do know tends to be based on personal experience. We have observed the erratic, unpredictable behaviors of addicted people and we form subjective impressions. When we are pulled into the orbit of someone who is addicted, our emotions take over. Earlier impressions such as: "This person is really impossible to be around. I hope it never happens to us," are now replaced with "I can't believe this is happening to us! This is horrible! What are we going to do?" Fear and anxiety take over. Rational thinking and clear perspective are lost.

Once our loved one gets into treatment, and even beforehand if possible, it is important to do some reading about the disease nature of chemical dependence. Personal observation, experience and hearsay do not suffice. They can make us even more anxious and upset. Once we are convinced that addiction is a disease of the brain, emotions and spirit, our negative emotions give way to the positive attitudes of hope, faith, compassion and forgiveness.

There is no lack of books and articles about addiction. Many of them are personal memoirs. Others are theoretical attempts at reducing a highly complex phenomenon to a simple set of axioms. Some books are valuable. Others are misleading and potentially harmful. Because there are so many options out there, I choose not to recommend specific titles. I do suggest that before you take the time to read a book about addiction, check the reviews and get an idea about whether the author has an axe to grind and whether her theories (if applicable) are based upon scientific and medical data. And before you spend any money or your valuable time on a book, use the Internet judiciously to learn what you can about the subject. Visit the National Institute on Drug Abuse (NIDA) website. Read their articles and explanations about substance use disorders and the opioid epidemic. Watch some videos featuring the NIDA Director Dr. Nora Volkow, an exceptionally gifted teacher and lecturer. Then visit the Substance Abuse and Mental Health Services Administration (SAMHSA) website for further information about addiction, treatment and co-occurring disorders, the common condition where chemical dependence co-occurs with mental illness. Perhaps at some point your loved one began to use drugs or alcohol as a way of self medicating a severe anxiety or depression condition. Or perhaps the severe drug use led to the development of a mental health disorder. Either way, the SAMHSA website is a useful tool for building a deeper understanding of the problems.

Armed with that deeper understanding, family and friends will then be better equipped to find acceptance and compassion for their loved one. This indeed ought to be a focus of their internal work while they await their loved one's return from treatment. It is also their work after the treatment episode ends. Finding compassion and understanding for our addicted loved ones is a lifelong task. The emotional and spiritual rewards make the process worthwhile.

Chapter 7

ADDICTION, COMPASSION AND FORGIVENESS

The absence of a loved one who is undergoing inpatient rehab is also an opportunity to do some soul searching and find ways to achieve forgiveness. But let's not put the cart before the horse. True forgiveness can only follow compassion and empathy toward the addicted individual. That requires an awareness of addiction as a disease. Otherwise we wind up pretending to forgive someone without understanding the nature of his condition.

If we hold on to the old Moral Model in which we judge the addicted person as weak and morally defective, we are unable to empathize with him. Once we clear away that false notion, we can set forth on the road to compassion and forgiveness.

Rabbi Akiba taught: "Do not judge your fellow until you have stood in his place, (Pirkei Avot 2:5)." Because it is impossible to become another person or to experience what it is like to stand in his shoes, Rabbi Akiba is essentially asking us not to be judgmental of others. Period. All the more so are we warned against pronouncing judgment on things and people we do not understand.

Imagine that you are in excellent physical shape, a superb athlete, carrying no excess weight. You take the time to exercise every day and you watch your diet carefully. You have a brother who is the opposite. He is obese, hardly ever exercises, regularly gorges himself with potato chips and ice cream. His doctor continually warns him of the risk of heart attack or stroke but he appears to pay no heed. He keeps eating and sitting on the couch watching TV. You feel like tearing your hair out because no matter how much you try to cajole and noodge, he doesn't change his behaviors. And because you take your physical health so seriously, you cannot understand why he keeps neglecting his.

He may be in the Precontemplation or Contemplation Stage of Change regarding his health, but you expect him to be in either the Preparation or Action Stage. You believe you know what is best for him. No doubt, you love and care for him. You don't want him to get sick or die. But you have allowed yourself to become entrenched in judgment and frustration. When you look at or talk to him, all you see is an obese, indolent man lacking the motivation to get healthy. Because you are the opposite, you have trouble feeling what it must be like to be him. In fact, you don't even try to put yourself in his place. You're too far apart.

So too with people suffering from chemical dependence. Because their life style and choices may be so perplexing and erratic, their loved ones are prone to judging and condemning them rather than making the effort to understand their trouble. Once the loved ones have educated themselves and embraced the Disease Model, the judgments begin to fade. They realize that the addicted individual, like the one suffering from obesity, has been visited with a condition not of his choosing. Who really wants to struggle with obesity, especially when he sees others eating as much as they want with little adverse effect? Who wants to struggle with addiction when they see others using drugs or alcohol recreationally without becoming dependent?

I am continually moved by the High Holy Days theme of God's judgment and mercy. Rosh Hashanah is also known as *Yom Ha-Din*, the Day of Judgment. The liturgy imagines God occupying the throne of justice, reviewing mankind's deeds, including those of every individual. The *Unetane Tokef* prayer compares us to sheep who pass in front of the shepherd one by one for review. At the same time we are reminded by the liturgy, the liturgical poetry (called *piyyutim*) and midrashic references that upon hearing the contrite pleas of Israel, God is moved to arise from the throne of justice (*Kisei Ha-Din*) and sit on the throne of mercy (*Kisei Ha-Rahamim*). In fact, Rabbinic literature often highlights the tension between God's attributes of judgment and mercy, yet in the end, it is God's quality of mercy and compassion that prevails.

In the spirit of *imitatio dei*, we humans are taught to try to emulate God's ways and follow God's example in our dealings with others. The High Holy Days remind us that if God can shift from judgment to mercy, so can we. But because we are not godly, we have difficulty freeing ourselves from the shackles of judgmental attitudes, and the way we see our addicted loved ones is especially challenging in this respect. We slip into the pattern of criticizing their erratic and self-destructive behaviors while overlooking their terrible struggle. We focus on the "addict" and ignore the person behind the addiction who yearns to be free of his dependence. The ability to feel compassion and empathy can only arise once we understand that we are not the only ones who are struggling. Our addicted loved one is grappling with a powerful foe in a battle of life and death. Especially as he undergoes treatment, we and he pray that he will prevail. This is a time when compassion is called for. Judgment must be put aside as much as possible.

Once we make room in our hearts for compassion, forgiveness inevitably follows. Without compassion, forgiveness is impossible. Achieving some measure of forgiveness for the addicted individual while she is in treatment is a worthwhile, indeed necessary goal. It is a major component in the process of preparation for her eventual completion of treatment and return to the family.

We must pause here to make some cautionary remarks.

Having established that compassion results from family members' understanding of the Disease Model of addiction, we need to be careful to explain the context for forgiveness. That is, what exactly are we forgiving? The fact that our loved one developed an addiction, or the harm she may have done to us as a result? Too often we confuse the two. Embracing the Disease Model of addiction, we are fully sincere in believing that our loved one is no more responsible for her chemical dependence than a diabetic person for having diabetes. We are not forgiving the addiction, we are striving to forgive her for the wounds she caused *as a result* of the addiction. Those are two completely different things.

In Part One I discussed the applicability of *Teshuvah* to the recovery process. I pointed out that because *Teshuvah* is a response to sin, we must be careful to separate *Teshuvah* from the phenomenon of addiction and, instead, apply it to the 4th Step personal inventory (if applicable) when a person examines her character and deeds. In so doing, she is able to understand how she has wronged others as a result of her addiction, and she is then equipped to make amends and ask forgiveness for these wrongs. But to equate the addicted person's recovery journey with *Teshuva* implies that she is sinful by means of her addiction. This contradicts the Disease Model that we have embraced.

Once our loved one is situated in a rehab program, she is probably going through a 4th Step inventory (or something similar) at some point in her treatment. She is involved in her own personal work of learning how she has harmed herself and others. While she is undergoing this difficult task, her loved ones need to do their own inventory. They may be blaming the addicted individual for hurting them so much and so often. They may be blaming themselves for harming her or for failing to prevent her descent into addiction. Either way, her absence now presents a precious opportunity to learn forgiveness. This isn't easy, especially because she is not around to apologize in person.

Jewish rabbinic texts emphasize the necessity of appeasement and restitution as preconditions for forgiveness. These generally must be done in person. According to Maimonides (Mishneh Torah, Hilkhot Teshuvah 2:9), "transgressions between man and his fellow, such as hurting his fellow, or cursing his fellow, or stealing from him, etc., *those are never forgiven until he gives his fellow what he owes him and [his fellow] is appeased* (Italics mine). Even if he returned the money he owed his fellow, he must appease him and ask him to forgive him. Even if he only perturbed his fellow verbally, he must make amends and meet with him until he forgives him…"

Doesn't this sound like the ways the addicted person can hurt his friends or loved ones?

But now he is away, receiving treatment, on the path to recovery yet unable to physically present himself to make restitution and amends. Were we to take Maimonides' ruling literally, we would have to conclude that the wronged party is exempt from forgiving his addicted friend or relative until that person can show up in person to right the wrongs he had committed.

Obviously, this is not possible while he is in residential treatment.

An exception to the general rule is called for in this instance. If the wronged party must wait to forgive until the patient completes treatment, a key opportunity will be missed. The addicted individual will return home and immediately face a wall of resentment residual anger and mistrust for all that transpired before treatment. Without compassion and forgiveness, the relationship will remain damaged and the process of rebuilding the relationship will be all the more daunting.

However, if forgiveness in absentia can be achieved, the chances for rebuilding and repair are vastly improved. Even better, the opportunity for direct, face-to-face forgiveness comes if the treatment program includes a family component such as a family weekend. Ideally, upon leaving treatment the ex-patient will be impressed by the warmth and sincerity of his loved ones' reception. He will immediately perceive that he has been forgiven. He now knows that his loved ones have realized the nature of his addiction disease. With this new knowledge, he is now better equipped to forgive himself and his loved ones for misunderstanding or judging him. The prognosis for a renewed family bond is now bright.

So while the treatment is happening, the family ought to reframe the way appeasement and restitution can unfold. If the amends cannot be accomplished in person, they can occur in absentia. Granted, the addicted person may not be paying back money or apologizing in person, but he is making the herculean effort to get well by undergoing treatment. He is doing his part. His recovery work is a stand-in for making amends in person. Once his loved ones accept this, and once they have found compassion, they can now begin to forgive.

The Talmud (Yoma 86b) relates the following teaching of Rabbi Yose ben Judah: "When a man commits a transgression, he should be forgiven the first time, forgiven the second time, forgiven the third time, but not forgiven the fourth time, as it is said, 'Thus says the Lord, For three transgressions of Israel [I will forgive], but not for four (paraphrased from Amos 2:6)…'"

While in the throes of addiction, a person might commit the same transgression five or six or more times. It seems that if we are not required to forgive her after four transgressions, all the more so are we exempt from letting go of the resentments and grudges resulting from all the additional times she has hurt us.

But addiction is different. Because the condition is not a matter of choice, many of the hurts and harmful deeds must be considered, at least on some level, unwitting. The perpetrator should eventually reckon with the ways he has hurt others, but he is not entirely responsible because he may have acted under the compulsion of his disease. Knowing this, he can more easily forgive himself. And his loved ones must admit that he usually did not consciously intend to harm them. His addiction was the primary cause. Otherwise, he never would have behaved is such a hurtful fashion. With this in mind, his loved ones can more easily learn to forgive him.

Chapter 8

Experiencing Treatment

While the patient's loved ones are grappling with issues of compassion, forgiveness and acceptance, she is going through her own challenging process – especially if she is undergoing residential treatment.

In chapter 5 I discussed different types of treatment ranging from outpatient to inpatient programs. In all cases, the fundamental core of the work ought to be evidence-based clinical techniques that provide patients with the recovery tools they will need to succeed once they complete the program. The term "evidence-based" describes clinical practice that combines solid research findings with treatment strategies developed from patients' needs and preferences. These strategies have generated positive outcomes with other patients in similar situations.[1] Any program that does not offer evidence-based treatment methods is really providing pseudo-treatment. Such a program might attract patients with yoga, nature experiences, Torah and worship, music and art therapy, a swimming pool and basketball court, delicious cuisine and country club amenities. These elements may contribute to and enhance one's treatment and recovery process. But minus the core of evidence-based methods, everything else is largely window dressing. Worse, the lack of medically proven protocols can render harm to the patients by squandering an opportunity to help them initiate positive change. Now that they are finally ready to get help, instead they are being told how to achieve and sustain recovery without the necessary tools. They may have learned how to *daven* (pray) or do yoga exercises, but the basics of relapse prevention and positive coping skills are what they will need most once they exit treatment.

I have no problem with Jewish treatment centers that emphasize 12 Steps, Torah and Jewish values. I do have a problem with those programs that offer religion and self-help as ends in themselves

---

1   For a detailed discussion on evidence-based practices in addiction treatment see S. Glasner-Edwards and R.Rawson, "Evidence-based practices in addiction treatment: review and recommendations for public policy.", *Health Policy.* 2010; 97(2-3):93-104.

while excluding evidence-based practice. Examples include the following: programs that do not allow patients to receive MAT or provide transportation to MAT clinics, fail to educate their patients about the Disease Model and biology of addiction, avoid utilizing evidence-based models such as Cognitive Behavioral Therapy (CBT) and Motivational Interviewing (MI). In the guise of using Torah and Jewish spirituality to inspire commitment to change, they risk leaving their patients rootless, lacking a solid foundation for recovery and relapse prevention. This foundation is what patients really need the most. They can get Torah learning and worship at a synagogue, yoga at a yoga studio (or even a JCC), art therapy at an art studio. They have come to the program seeking *treatment*. Inpatient or outpatient, residential or not, the clinic must give them what they are looking for. That is its mandate. As the great sage Hillel said, "the rest is commentary…(Talmud Shabbat 31a)."

In my experience as a rehabilitation counselor, I often utilized CBT and MI with my patients. I enjoyed teaching CBT principles in psychoeducational groups and using MI techniques during individual counseling sessions. Many volumes and articles have been written about both models and it would be impossible to thoroughly describe them here. Let it suffice that CBT is an addictions treatment model that encourages patients to examine triggers (usually external factors, people or events that trigger thoughts of drug use), followed by the thoughts and accompanying feelings that lead to either positive or negative outcomes.[2] In the educational groups I would ask the patients to suggest their own triggers and run through how the negative thoughts and attitudes would lead to disturbing feelings that would in turn generate cravings and drug use. We would then work on reframing the original trigger into a positive thought and see how this could lead to a better outcome. This process is referred to in CBT talk as "Functional Analysis of Behavior."

Here's an example: When asked about what triggers him, Patient X points to his wife's suspicion that he is sneaking out of the house to use drugs with his friends at the bar. He is upset because he is maintaining sobriety and therefore feels unjustly accused. He thinks to himself: "I am trying my best to stay clean, nothing I do will make her trust me. I wish she'd just stay off my back!" The accompanying feelings are frustration, anger, disappointment bordering on despair.

---

2   See the SAMHSA article on CBT found online at https://www.integration.samhsa.gov/clinical-practice/sbirt/CBT_Overview_Part_1.pdf

Immediately, the cravings pop up. In the end he says to himself, "F_ _ _ it, I might as well go use because she'll never trust me anyway." The outcome: relapse.

Having gone through this exercise, I would then challenge X to come up with a different thought about the original trigger, his wife's suspicion. This is called reframing. I would love it when he, or someone else in the group would say: "Instead of focusing on my wife's mistrust, maybe she's suspicious because she loves me and cares about me and doesn't want to see me relapse." We would then review the accompanying feelings, which would generally be akin to reassurance, love, warmth, confidence in her care for him. With these feelings in tow, the likelihood of cravings and relapse would be diminished.

The patients always enjoyed this exercise and others like it. They felt empowered with the potential to rethink and reframe troublesome triggers. They experienced a sense of hope in their ability to avoid cravings. Once we practiced Functional Analysis exercises like this one, we would then be equipped to discuss topics like Refusal Skills, Coping with Cravings and Seemingly Irrelevant Decisions[3]. Armed with these newly learned tools, the patients would be better equipped to face the challenges awaiting them among their families, workplace, friends and the outside world in general.

It is difficult to imagine a treatment process that excludes an evidence- based practice like the one I just described. CBT is certainly not the only valid approach. It happens to be a particularly effective one. Whether they utilize CBT or not, treatment programs should employ approaches that have been proven medically and scientifically beneficial. Torah, yoga and guided meditation, helpful as they may be, cannot replace the fundamental core of evidence-based treatment models.

Motivational Interviewing (MI) is a technique that is based upon the person-centered approach originally developed by Carl Rogers over a half century ago. It is best described in a book of the same name by William Miller and Steven Rollnick.[4] Person-centered or humanistic treatment assumes that the patient often knows best what

---

3   The choices and acts that mask an unconscious desire to relapse, they often appear to be irrelevant and insignificant but can lead to harmful outcomes.

4   Miller and Rollnick, *Motivational Interviewing*.

he needs and what his goals ought to be.

MI is a short-term model where the professional tries to stimulate the patient's motivation by practicing active listening, showing empathy, gently challenging discrepancies between the patient's behaviors and goals. It is up to the patient to define these goals; it is not the counselor's role to define it for him. MI heavily relies on the Transtheoretical Model of Change that I have been referring to often in this volume. If a patient is in the Precontemplation Stage, the counselor tries to stimulate some doubt and questioning by asking open rather than closed questions (e.g. "What do you think about your problem?" instead of "Do you think you have a problem?"). The goal is to encourage the patient to develop a rapport with the professional and eventually talk more openly and discover the motivation to change.

I used MI frequently while meeting individually with patients. I received intensive training in this model and I enjoyed applying it to my practice. I found it to be effective. I noticed that, because it encouraged self-efficacy among patients, the outcomes tended to be positive. Patients were able to change behaviors not because someone told them to but because they came to the realization themselves (with some professional prodding, that is). I always felt gratification when I witnessed the self-motivated shifts and changed behaviors and attitudes among my patients.

Can this be achieved by Torah study, prayer or yoga? Perhaps, but I haven't seen any hard data to support this. Rather, the evidence-based practices are the essential backbone of treatment and recovery. Everything else is a corollary.

Earlier in Part One, Chapter 9, I discussed the problematic use of *Teshuvah* with regard to treatment. *Teshuvah* certainly has its place in recovery as the addicted person makes a positive turn towards engaging in a spiritual inventory to see how she has hurt herself and others. But applying *Teshuvah* in broad terms to addiction and recovery can confuse the Moral with the Medical Model. I suggested that Jewish treatment centers and professionals exercise care and caution in how they use the term *Teshuvah*. It is not the same as recovery. It is part of recovery as the individual exercises soul searching and makes the necessary amends.

I suggest two safer and more accurate Hebrew terms for Jewish recovery: *Refuah* and *Tikkun*. *Refuah* means "healing." In the standard *Mi-sheberakh* prayer, the spiritual leader and/or congregation pray for *refuat ha-nefesh u'rfuat ha-guf* – healing of soul and healing of body for the afflicted. Typically, names of family and friends of the supplicant are added to the *Misheberakh* list. Some are suffering acute illness, others struggle with chronic conditions. Because addiction is considered a chronic brain disease with spiritual dimensions, it is surely appropriate to add names of our addicted loved ones to the *Misheberakh* list, all the while respecting their privacy if needed. I'm sure many addicted people would welcome their inclusion in the prayers of the community; others would prefer to remain anonymous. That, of course, is their right.

The prayer essentially includes all those who are ill, without distinction or limit. It invokes the names of the Patriarchs (and, in some versions, the Matriarchs) in order to emphasize the idea that we pray for divine help solely on our own merit but on the merit of our ancestors. The *Misheberakh* then includes the name(s) of our loved ones and implores God to strengthen and heal them and show them mercy. How moving to imagine a community joining together to invoke God's name on behalf of those who are sick and suffering! Addicted individuals are suffering too and are deserving of our prayers.

In this context, *refuah* makes perfect sense. *Refuah* and recovery are one and the same. As the addicted individual travels along her recovery path, her brain and her soul are undergoing a powerful healing process. Some of the healing is clearly evident through her affect, attitudes and behavior. Much of the healing is beneath the surface, both physically and spiritually. That is where *tikkun* comes in. The broken shards of the soul and the physical and mental damage caused by the addicted life are being repaired. The neglected body and spirit are now receiving the proper attention. The patient in treatment feels relief from the punishing cycle of drug or alcohol use. Even if she is not totally abstinent once the treatment episode is over, or even if she replaces her drug of choice with another drug without developing dependence, her mind and soul are experiencing healing and repair.

I prefer *refuah* and *tikkun* as recovery terms because they encompass the formerly addicted person's own healing process. They focus on the present and the hope of a brighter future. They remove the pejorative tone of sin and transgression alluded to in *Teshuvah*.

They even out the playing field of disease by including addicted people within the numbers of those who are experiencing all types of serious illness. The emphasis on healing and repair helps remove the stigma of addiction.

I would hope that Jewish treatment centers consider employing the concepts of *refuah* and *tikkun* in their programs while exercising caution about how they talk about *teshuvah*. *Teshuva* can play a vital role when identified with *heshbon ha-nefesh*, spiritual inventory. If the program is 12 Step oriented, *teshuvah* will automatically come into play during the treatment process.

As I have noted earlier, the 12 Step philosophy can be problematic for certain individuals. It is not for everyone. One of the limitations of 12 Step programs is its adherents' tendency to espouse the 12 Step approach as the only valid path to recovery, specifically its abstinence-based outlook. I have long believed that recovery is an individualized and idiosyncratic phenomenon. The recovering individual is entitled to set his own unique recovery path. No one else should have the authority to tell him what his recovery process ought to be. Those who accept the 12 Step approach are choosing for themselves and are thus subject to the wisdom and suggestions of that program. All well and good. But those who choose an alternative approach need not be judged or criticized for opting out of the 12 Steps or following a Harm Reduction model. If they are able to reduce their alcohol intake from 12 beers to 2 per day, who has the right to question their recovery? Why should 12 Step veterans feel justified using the pejorative term "dry drunk" when referring to a sober person who doesn't "have program" (12 Steps) or still shows signs of the "isms" (like alcoholism) while staying sober?

My college training in cultural anthropology, as well as life experiences, taught me to respect other cultures and perspectives outside of my own. This holds true for addiction and recovery. I choose not to judge or criticize anyone who is trying to change, even when the strategy and tactics would differ from my own. I'm not necessarily the one who knows best. Every person has the right to determine his own recovery path. He can surely benefit from treatment professionals, people in recovery and 12 Step veterans. But in the end, it is the addicted individual who must select and follow his own road to recovery.

Jewish treatment centers can help by ensuring that evidence-based models are employed. Ancillary enhancements such as Torah study, worship and practice of *Gemilut Hasadim* (deeds of lovingkindness) ought never to serve as replacements for basic treatment and should not be confused with treatment. They can be wonderful adjuncts but there is little hard data to show their effectiveness with long-term outcomes.

Moreover, 12 Step approaches ought to be considered in the same light as the religious activities listed above. As I have mentioned earlier, the 12 Steps present a solid framework for recovery that has helped millions throughout the past several decades. But they are not for everyone. Though they were originally referred to as the "12 **Suggested** Steps" in the "Alcoholics Anonymous" volume, they have become canonized by devotees in AA and NA. This leaves little room for accepting and tolerating variant recovery approaches, including the Harm Reduction Model. Many 12 Steppers have difficulty accepting the idea that a person who cuts down on her drinking and drugging can still be in her own version of recovery. I would like to see evidence of this more open recovery model in Jewish treatment centers.

Several rabbis and addiction specialists before me have taken great pains to demonstrate how the 12 Steps are consistent with Jewish teachings. Their contributions have been valuable. But it is time for Jewish treatment professionals to investigate and develop new ways to enhance treatment. The ethical and spiritual dimensions of the 12 Step Philosophy have precursors in earlier schools of Jewish moral and religious development. One good example is the *Mussar* Movement. *Mussar* has it's beginnings in Biblical ethical teachings as developed by the Sages in "Pirkei Avot" (Sayings of the Fathers) and other works. The moral principles of *Mussar* continued to evolve in medieval works by Sa'adia Gaon (10th century) and Bahya ibn Pakuda (11th-12th century) and culminated in the teachings of Rabbi Israel Salanter in the 19th century. R. Salanter was able to turn *Mussar* teachings into a movement, one that emphasized spiritual and ethical practices that were personalized and adapted for the needs of each individual. *Mussar* has been particularly notable for its profound insights on the nature of the *yetser ha-ra* (evil inclination) and how it can be worked with and turned around for good purposes.[5]

The *Mussar* philosophy has immense potential as a valuable tool for spiritual and moral growth in Jewish treatment settings. Rather

---

5   Greg Marcus, "What is Mussar? A history and overview of the virtues-based approach to Jewish Ethics," found online at https://www.myjewishlearning.com/article/the-musar-movement/

than continuing to automatically impose 12 Step models whose origins were extraneous to Judaism, Jewish treatment professionals might consider adapting an indigenously Jewish approach such as *Mussar* as an enhancement to treatment.

Finally, a word about Jewish treatment centers and MAT. As I have indicated, a residential program that shuns MAT for opioid dependent patients is out of step with medical treatment protocols. Sadly, such programs are in the majority. According to a NIDA funded study, less than 50% of privately funded rehab programs offer MAT, and only 1/3 of opioid dependent patients at these programs receive MAT. Therefore, Jewish treatment programs that withhold MAT from opioid dependent patients are in good company.

That doesn't make it OK. Nor does it serve the needs and interests of the patients, many of whom face bleaker outcomes without the aid of MAT. If they have been compelled to detox off methadone or buprenorphine in order to stay in an inpatient rehab, their tolerance for opioids decreases the longer they are in the program. Once they leave, the risk of overdose resulting from relapse increases because their tolerance has become low.

So what to do? Are Jewish treatment centers expected to directly provide MAT for those who need it? The answer is no. Should they make it possible for those with severe opioid disorders to receive medication for stabilization, if they so choose, and to increase their safety? The answer, in my opinion, is yes. Once the program conducts an assessment and evaluation and determines a diagnosis of opioid dependence, if the patient is admitted, she ought to be offered the medication she needs upon request. This doesn't require installing a methadone dispensary or even brining in MD's who are trained buprenorphine prescribers. It simply means that the program will offer access to MAT clinics in the community. Patients would be transported whenever necessary to these clinics to receive their medication (methadone or naltrexone) or prescription (Buprenorphine/ Suboxone). Take-home bottles of methadone or Suboxone meds would be held in safe keeping by a staff member at the residential facility and administered daily to the patient. It's as simple as that.

Or, once the initial evaluation assigns the diagnosis of opioid dependence, the facility has another option. If, for whatever reason, it chooses not to provide any option for MAT despite the patient's wishes, it should deny admission and make an appropriate referral to a program that offers MAT. This applies specifically to the diagnoses of Opioid Use Disorders, Moderate or Severe. In most cases, such diagnoses warrant the use of MAT for better outcomes. If the diagnoses is Opioid Use Disorder, Mild, MAT may not be the best course of treatment because the disease has not progressed enough to justify MAT. The program may decide that it can offer a solid, evidence-based treatment for this patient without the use of medication. The bottom line: the patient's interests and needs are what matter most. Jewish treatment programs must acknowledge this and act accordingly. If the patient's rehabilitation needs are inconsistent with the program's philosophy, the program is ethically bound to refer the patient elsewhere.

Chapter 9

TERMINATION AND TRANSITION

The treatment episode is about to end. In the case of residential rehab, a major transition lies ahead. This applies both to the patient and her family. The goal is to effect as smooth a transition as possible.

Most professions have their own system of ethics. Addiction counseling is no exception. One of the ethical principles I learned long ago may sound somewhat strange but it makes perfect sense: In any treatment situation, termination should be discussed either at or near the beginning of the treatment episode. One might wonder, isn't this jumping the gun? Shouldn't the patient be given a chance to see how she is progressing before thinking about what may follow?

With the exception of Medication Assisted Treatment, most programs offer relatively short-term interventions. State funded inpatient programs tend to run 28-45 days depending upon insurance limits. Some can last three months or more, depending on several factors. Privately run programs vary in length. In any case, the treatment will not last indefinitely. The patient needs to have an indication of what might happen after termination. Will she step down to an outpatient program? Where will she live? Is a sober living situation recommended? What about issues such as family reunification and employment? All these matters should be reviewed early in the treatment episode because the treatment is framed within the patient's short and long-term goals. These goals intersect with the patient's immediate future after treatment. If she begins to process this near the beginning of the treatment episode the transition after termination is more likely to be successful.

Here's a biblical parallel. After the exodus from Egypt, Moses leads his people Israel to Mt. Sinai. He then proceeds to ascend the mountain, knowing little about what will transpire up there and how long he will be absent. He fails to adequately prepare the people for his absence. No interim plan is discussed. We learn in the Book of Exodus that Moses stays on the mountain 40 days and nights. He spends that time communing with God and receiving the 10 Commandments. According to the traditional view, God also issued

Moses the teachings of the Written Torah (5 Books of Moses) and Oral Torah (Mishnah and Talmud) during that period. One cannot begin to imagine the intensity of this experience for Moses. But something important seemed to have been missing.

Not only does Moses neglect to properly brief his people Israel before his departure, but God lets Moses down in a key way. Knowing that Moses would eventually have to descend the mountain to return to the people, signifying a return to reality, God ought to have briefed Moses at or near the beginning of the 40-day period. God could have told him something like, "This extended time you are spending with Me will come to an end and you're going to have to get back to the real world. Just know, when that time comes, you're not going to like what your people have been doing in your absence. They're going to build a Golden Calf. Since you didn't warn them before you left that you'd be lingering up here for more than just a few days, and since you didn't set up a solid contingency plan for leadership, surely you can understand why the people would become so disoriented and lost. They've been relying on you, and as far as they know, you may have disappeared up here on the mountain. So please have some compassion and control your temper when you see what they've done. And forgive your brother Aaron for giving in to pressure by building the idol."

But the Torah records no such conversation between God and Moses. God neglected to discuss a termination plan that would take effect once the 40-day Sinai episode would conclude. And the result? A poor transition. Moses descended the mountain after 40 days, saw the people worshiping the Golden Calf, immediately lost his temper and smashed the two tablets of the Ten Commandments. Three thousand people were slain by the Levites, and the Lord inflicted a plague upon the people.[1] Not a good outcome. It could have been otherwise, had both Moses and God planned differently.

For the patient, a residential rehab experience lasting a month or more is intense and outside the norm of daily life. He is now abstinent and is no longer intimate with his best friend, his drug of necessity. His brain, body and soul are undergoing a rapid adjustment and transformation. He gets up every morning, attends groups and individual therapy, gets fed, exercises, starts to tend to his physical, emotional and spiritual needs on a 24/7 basis. His life is dramatically

---

1 Exodus 32:15-29.

and *temporarily* altered. It is as if he is standing on Mount Sinai, communing with something infinitely greater, existing in an alternate reality. But this experience is of limited duration, and he must be given proper preparation for the time when the episode will end and he will return to a more normalized daily life. That is why termination must be discussed at or near the beginning of the treatment episode.

And what about the family? How can the family be adequately prepared for his return? In Chapter 6, I offered tips for shoring up spiritual resources and inner preparedness. But there is more. As the rehab period nears conclusion, the family ought to be addressing additional considerations, some concrete and some attitudinal. Here are a few tips:

1. Keep going to Al-Anon. Get more perspective on the limits of your ability to change and mold the addicted individual in your image. Learn more about how you can detach from the person and the situation in a healthy and loving way. If you don't like the meetings you've been attending go to a different meeting, but don't give up.

2. If he will be living with you, be sure to remove alcoholic beverages from your home. Lock up any prescription meds that have abuse potential.

3. If he will be living with you, work up some guidelines and establish some boundaries that will ensure a smoother and conflict-free transition. For example, if you and he are favorably disposed towards AA or NA, set a standard for regular and consistent meeting attendance. Curfews may be a setup for disappointment, but it is still a good idea to ask him to be home by the time you go to sleep unless he is working night hours. If he is coming home in the middle of the night, you have every right to question what he is doing out there. You know you can't control him or what he does, but you need to have safe boundaries and you don't want an actively relapsing person living under your roof.

4. If he will be living in a sober house, begin thinking about how often you will see him or communicate by phone or email. Setting limits here is also a good idea. This also applies to the nature and content of the communication. If he is reaching

out to you only when he wants something from you, this is manipulative behavior that needs to be addressed.

5. Returning to the biblical parallel, you are certainly not God and he is not Moses, but you want to be sharply attuned to the challenges he will face once he returns to the real world. Assuming you are in touch with him during his treatment episode, begin talking with him about setting parameters upon his completion of treatment. He is about to "come down the mountain" after a special, almost surrealistic experience. He will encounter pitfalls and obstacles once he returns to the real world. He might be existing in what is called the "pink cloud" of early recovery, when he is highly confident and gratified by his success in achieving abstinence. The pink cloud can delude him into becoming overconfident and, hence, more vulnerable to relapse. He will need you to remind him that danger lurks from inside and outside him. Even though he is changing and healing through recovery, he will probably have vestiges of addictive thinking and urges, and the world out there can present multiple temptations. Which leads to the next tip…

6. The words "people, places, things" are frequently cited in treatment and 12 Step settings. This refers to *changing* people, places and things. The person in recovery knows he needs to shift his social environment away from drug using acquaintances. He needs to avoid places where drugs are sold, or bars, or places that he associates with his previous life in addiction. At first he may be able to stick with ordering a coke in a bar but eventually he may wind up asking the bartender to add a shot of rum, or he may start indulging in *real* coke of the powder variety. And he needs to change things such as discarding any paraphernalia that may have been hidden and avoiding objects that may trigger new cravings, such as matches, beer mugs, flip cellphones or whatever he used beforehand to support his addiction. One of the great blessings of 12 Step fellowships is their success in providing a ready made social group for anyone wishing to find sober friends and a new support system.

Part Two – Lifting the Fog

In the biblical story of Cain and Abel (Genesis, chapter 4), Cain is crestfallen after God favors Abel's sacrifice over his own. God responds by trying to both comfort, motivate and warn Cain: "Why are you distressed, and why is your face fallen? Surely, if you do right, there is uplift. But if you do not do right, sin couches at the door; Its urge is toward you, yet you can be its master (Genesis 4:6-7)." God sees that Cain is standing at the threshold of change. He is faced with the choice of doing well or missing the mark (Hebrew *hait*, translated here as *sin*). The object of sin lies in wait and sends off a magnetic signal to tempt the "sinner". But he has the power to ward it off and master it.

The addicted individual started out making bad choices by using certain drugs. Eventually the drug became his master. Once he attains recovery, the drug is still out there and, in Biblical terms, its urge is towards him. Step 1 of the 12 Steps suggests he is powerless over the drug or alcohol. This may or may not be true. He may find he has more control over his ability to avoid the drug than he imagines. But the drug doesn't go away, and it beckons to him. The treatment episode has hopefully taught him how to successfully cope with the cravings and urges. But now that he is returning to the real world, the temptations are also real and the opportunities to relapse abound.

In a midrashic commentary on Genesis 4:7, Rabbi Isaac taught: "At first it [sin] is like a passing visitor, then like a guest who stays longer, and finally like the master of the house (Genesis Rabbah 22:6)." He might as well have been writing about the insidious way casual drug use can turn into dependence and addiction.[2] However, it is different for the newly recovering person, especially one who has recently completed treatment. For her, the risks of relapse are exceedingly high, even if she is on a pink cloud and believes her recovery is solid. If she picks up again, the drug will not start out like a passing visitor or even a longer term guest. It will most likely overtake and master her from the outset. Her brain receptors and reward system will immediately be reactivated based on her past experiences with the drug, and it will be off to the races. Depending on the type of drug, she will be at risk for overdose. At the very least, she stands to lose much of what she gained in treatment. As I mentioned earlier, relapse is not so much a

---

2   A reminder: It is not my intention to equate "sin" in the midrash with the phenomenon of addiction (as a moral judgment) but only with the way drug use can take over a person's life.

part of recovery as a symptom of the disease. And it is a symptom that can be devastating.

If the family members see themselves as her support system, they must do all they can to remove as many obstacles to her recovery as possible once she returns from treatment. It is *not* their role to control, manage or interfere with her recovery. It *is* their role to hold her hand and help her walk along the obstacle-strewn path of recovery. Obviously this does not apply to cases where the family members have needed to effect a solid boundary separating them from the addicted individual. I believe these cases are more the exception than the rule. More often, there will be a renewal of contact and communication once the treatment is over. This can present a daunting and challenging opportunity for both parties. But the rewards can be immensely gratifying for all concerned.

Part Three

RECOVERY AND RETURN

Chapter 1

INTO THE WILDERNESS

The treatment episode has ended. A period of adjustment begins. For the recovering individual, the pink cloud may linger for a while. It will eventually give way to a rude awakening: recovery can be tough and fraught with obstacles. For his family, the hopes and expectations that flourished while he was in treatment may begin to diminish as the family realizes that, although he is getting better, the process of change doesn't necessarily happen overnight.

According to the Stages of Change model, the Action Stage can last well beyond the actual treatment phase. It generally continues for about six months. This means that the 4-6 week treatment episode constitutes only the first part of the Action Stage. The remaining months are marked by the recovering person's efforts to employ the tools he learned in rehab. The actions he takes to continue getting well are by no means automatic yet. They require conscious intention, dedication and commitment. He knows this better than anyone else. His family would do well to come alongside him and acknowledge how hard the work is for him. It is as if he had recent surgery for a broken limb and must undergo rehab and physical therapy to regain proper functioning. No one can expect this to happen quickly or effortlessly. It takes daily exercise and the determination to persist even when the benefits and progress seem elusive.

Think of the person emerging from active addiction and rehab as akin to the Israelites who were freed from Egyptian bondage after years of suffering. Suddenly they find themselves a free people. Eventually they will be provided with the Torah, a structure of living, by Moses the lawgiver. But even then, they have difficulty navigating their newly found freedom.

How do we know this? The Torah describes their frequent doubting, complaining and backsliding. Who can blame them? Life in slavery is all they have known. Now they are expected to instantly adjust to life in freedom. That is not a fair or reasonable expectation.

Trapped at the Sea of Reeds with the Egyptian army approaching, the people are panicked and desperate. Their voices dripping with sarcasm, they challenge Moses: There weren't enough graves in Egypt that you had to lead us here to die in the desert?" (Exodus 14:10-12.) Then, after being miraculously rescued, they panic again when they face thirst and starvation. They tell Moses that they long to return to Egypt so they can once again eat all the foods to which they were accustomed (Exodus 16:2-3). First, they build a Golden Calf (Exodus 32), then they complain about Moses' leadership and stage a rebellion under Korah (Numbers 16). They adopt the licentious ways of the Moabites (Numbers 25:1-5). They refuse to be heartened by the positive reports of Joshua and Caleb in the incident of the spies (Numbers 13-14), and instead they choose to be infected by the negativity of the other 10 spies, believing that they will never have the power to overtake the Canaanites. Thus, they are doomed to wander in the wilderness for forty years, only to perish in the desert before their children can enter the Promised Land.

I imagine I would have been one of them. Like them, I would have been plagued with doubts, fear and uncertainty. Like them, the recovering individual struggles with the reality and challenges of a newly found freedom. And his biggest fear? Failure and relapse.

Chemical dependence is a chronic, relapsing disease. While the disease is in early remission, even after treatment is over, the risk of relapse is significant. This can last for up to a year, even into what is called the Maintenance Stage of change. According to NIDA, relapse doesn't mean treatment has failed. Good treatment plants seeds of recovery and helps to reorient thinking. Solid treatment experiences help bring physical, spiritual and emotional healing. If the recovery process gets derailed, this does not mean treatment was for naught. Every good treatment episode contributes to the long-term path of recovery.

Relapses are common. So are slips. What's the difference?

In general, a slip means the recovering individual, while still committed to her recovery plan, has an episode of drug or alcohol use but is able to stop quickly and resume the plan. For example, Sarah concludes treatment, returns home, goes back to work and is doing well. Her drug of choice, alcohol, has been out of her life for a few months. She is attending 12 Step meetings and trying hard to maintain sobriety. Then, while attending a family gathering and feeling somewhat anxious and intimidated, she is offered a glass of wine. Though she had intended to avoid any alcohol at the event, she succumbs to temptation and accepts the glass. She may wind up drinking a second or third. Once the gathering is over she feels terrible about what she has done. She wonders whether she has negated all the progress she achieved during and immediately after treatment. She then renews her commitment to stay sober.

Sarah went through a slip, not a full blown relapse. Had she accepted a line of cocaine or a pill at the party it still would have constituted a slip as long as she returned to abstinence, because in her case abstinence from all drugs was part of her recovery plan. And Sarah is far from alone. Her slip was a symptom of the addiction disease. It doesn't disappear so readily in most people.

Relapse generally refers to either a planned resumption of heavy use or an unplanned slip that progresses into continued use. Relapses can be devastating and life threatening. They are also common for people in early recovery. No wonder they and their family members are so afraid of it. Fear of relapse can darken an otherwise cheerful and hopeful recovery. In itself, this fear can make one even more vulnerable, as if to say, "I can't deal with the fear so I might as well just pick up." The family members also walk around worrying that their loved one could relapse. When everyone lives in fear, the risk of negative outcomes is elevated.

Here is where trust comes into play. The family may have reached a level of compassion and forgiveness for themselves and their addicted loved one. However, rebuilding trust can be a tall order, a formidable task. I would often share the following situation with my patients in group: Imagine you are working hard stay sober. You're doing all the right things. One day your wife tells you: "I left a $20 bill on the dresser and now it's not there. Have you seen it? You didn't take it did you?" You immediately feel accused. You believe she doesn't trust you and thinks you took the cash to buy drugs. The first thought in your mind: "Well, I'll never gain her trust no matter how hard I try, so I might as well go out and use anyway." But as you think the matter through, you reframe her accusation and tell her: "I know it's going to be hard me to rebuild trust with you because of all I did to you before. So I'm willing to keep trying to stay sober and work hard so you can trust me again. And, by the way, I didn't take the $20."

Whether the recovering individual is back home or elsewhere, family members are probably going to be on guard, careful and watchful. Actions, speech and attitudes will be closely scrutinized by both parties. As the broken relationships are being repaired, the healing process will be rocky. Any expectation that the path will be smooth is a pipe dream.

Here's my suggestion for family members: Be patient. Continue to learn and practice healthy detachment. Don't expect miracles. Be mindful of how you think and what crosses your lips. You have the power to provide immense love and support at a most vulnerable time for your newly recovering loved one. You also have the power to help derail the healing process. Always think before you speak.

My suggestion for the person in recovery: Be patient with yourself and with others. Remember that you spent months and years of your life doing harm to yourself, and in the process you hurt your loved ones too. You didn't really mean to do that. Many of your harmful actions resulted from your addiction condition. You never wanted the addiction, you didn't choose it, though you may not be responsible for having the disease you're still accountable for your actions. You still need to reckon with the effects of the addiction and its harmful impact on others. This is why members of 12 Step programs endeavor to take a *heshbon ha-nefesh*, a spiritual and moral inventory as part of working the steps. The people around you are not going to immediately be able to trust you. Some of them may even want to avoid you. You may notice that those who don't avoid you still seem uncomfortable around you. That's OK and to be expected. Give them, and yourself, time.

After leading his people forty years in the desert, Moses still had trouble trusting them and accepting their shortcomings and lack of faith. As told in the Book of Numbers, he loses his temper at the people when they complain of lack of water. Instead of following God's order to speak to the rock he strikes it, berates the people and fails to sanctify God. As a result, God informs him he will not cross over the Jordan River to lead the people into the Promised Land (Numbers 20:2-13). After so many years, Moses is still unable to understand and tolerate the peoples' faults.

At the same time the people, having been given so many chances only to slip back into their old attitudes, cannot rise above their fear and lack of trust of Moses and God. But like Moses, they refuse to give up. They stay in the relationship, however tenuous it may be. Similarly, the newly recovering individual and his family need to have faith in themselves and one another, despite the pitfalls, slips and misunderstandings. They need to stay in the game to heal the relationship. The effort is great but the rewards considerable.

Chapter 2

REENTERING THE CAMP

The Torah portions Tazria/Metzora (Leviticus 12-15) include detailed descriptions of the disease called *Tzara'at* (often translated as leprosy), its diagnosis by the priest, the mandatory period of quarantine and the process of restoring the leper to his camp and his tent. Rabbis and sages throughout the centuries have pondered the meaning of this section and why the Torah chose to describe it in such meticulous detail. Though the Torah does not explicitly suggest the cause of this disease, the Sages sought to impose a moral dimension on it. They used wordplay to connect the Hebrew word for leper (*Metzora*) with the Hebrew for slander (*Motzi Ra*) to teach the lesson that leprosy is caused by the sin of slander.[1] This is an exegetical interpretation and was most likely not the intent of the author of Leviticus. But it allowed rabbis the opportunity to preach against gossip, slander and the destructive potential of the evil tongue. Contemporary rabbis still bring moral lessons to Tazria/Metzora. The text is sufficiently unappealing and technical to cause teachers to search for any creative ideas and interpretations that will bring some relevance to these forbidding passages.

During the escalation of the HIV/AIDS epidemic in the 1990s, many synagogue rabbis (including myself) used Tazria/Metzora as an opportunity to connect the Torah portions with myths and prejudice about the disease. We addressed the social isolation of virus carriers, intolerance against homosexuality, ignorance about how the virus was contracted and passed on. As society became better educated about the epidemic, the language of ignorance and intolerance gradually gave way to more open and enlightened attitudes. Virus carriers and people with full-blown AIDS began to feel more comfortable disclosing their plight, and treatment become more affordable and available.

Once we fully understood that HIV/AIDS isn't contagious through casual contact we found it easier to stop avoiding those who were stricken. Once we learned to accept homosexuality as a different but equal form of sexual identity, we stopped shunning the LGBTQ

---

1   This teaching is found in the Midrash Leviticus Rabbah 16:1.

community. Laws and social mores reflected changing attitudes. Gays and lesbians were accepted to rabbinical schools and welcomed into synagogues. The long period of isolation ended.

Leviticus chapter 14 describes the rituals enacted once a person with *Tzara'at* was deemed cured. The priest would exit the camp and examine the leper. If the skin had sufficiently healed, the priest would perform a ritual of purification and the recovered person could re-enter the camp. He would be required to remain outside his tent for an additional seven days, after which he would shave all his hair, bathe, wash his clothes, present a sacrifice at entrance to the Tent of Meeting, and the priest would enact another ritual involving oil and sacrificial blood. Only then could the cured leper return to his tent.

Why the elaborate rituals? The leper had experienced the discomfort, pain and social stigma of his disease. Notwithstanding the moralizing of the Sages, the Torah attaches no ethical etiology to *Tzara'at*. All we know is the person was afflicted and then had to be quarantined. The purpose of the quarantine was to protect the population lest the disease be infectious. The individual was not being punished for any wrongdoing. Yet he was forced to leave his home and community for an extended period while hoping and praying for a cure. Doesn't this sound like addiction and rehab?

The recovering leper's prayers were answered. His skin ailment was healing and he could now think about returning home. Yet he had undergone a severe trauma. As far as he knew, his disease could have been incurable. While in isolation, he had no idea whether he would ever be able to rejoin his family. Like Jonah, existing in the belly of the great fish, all he could do was pray and wait. And now that the cure had arrived, rituals were needed to mark the end of a traumatic episode and the beginning of a new lease on life. In the context of ancient society, a sacrificial rite involving animals, birds, blood and water was deemed necessary. This is what held meaning for the participants, a ceremony that enabled the recovered leper to undergo purification and express gratitude to God. Without the ritual, the transition from isolation to society would have been more difficult. The trauma itself as well as its resolution had to be acknowledged in ritual fashion.

So too, when the person recovering from addiction leaves the social quarantine of inpatient rehab, having been removed from family and friends for a period of healing and treatment, she faces a transitional moment that is profoundly important. How can she both celebrate and commemorate it? She has undergone the severe trauma of her addiction and has emerged from its spiritual fog. This great achievement should be recognized in some way. But how?

Her previous life in addiction was isolating. Her return to her family and closest friends ought to be the opposite: a return to connectivity with those nearest and dearest to her. The fog of addiction had engulfed her; now that her mind, body and spirit are starting to work together again her life can be enriched by rebuilding relationships. Therefore, any recognition of her successful completion of treatment should involve a limited number of key people. Not a public ceremony. The leper's ritual of purification and re-entry to the camp and his tent were accomplished in the presence of the priest. It was not a community-wide celebration.

If the recovering individual feels a connection with Judaism, she may want to reach out to a rabbi. Just as the person traumatized by leprosy needs the intervention of a priest to effect purification and re-entry, the person in early recovery could benefit from establishing contact with clergy. If she is a member of a synagogue, the congregation's rabbi might be the obvious choice. However, this is not a given. It is essential that the rabbi be someone with whom she enjoys a good rapport, a non-judgmental presence. Whether she turns to her synagogue rabbi or someone else, her purpose is to set up time with the rabbi to process and reflect on her past regrets, accomplishments in treatments, and immediate goals in early recovery. The therapeutic and spiritual value of such an encounter could be significant.

The recovering leper was required to undergo a ritual of purification before returning to the camp and his tent. The recovering addicted person ought to think about how she could incorporate some ritual ceremony to mark her return to her community. This is where recruiting the input of a rabbi could be valuable. The ceremony would most likely be private, unless she is the rare kind of person who feels comfortable acknowledging her addiction and recovery in public, in front of her synagogue community. In the private ceremony, she and the rabbi could recite Psalms related to healing (e.g. Psalm 30, 91 or 121). The rabbi would recite a *mi-sheberakh* prayer of healing for her. She could write down a brief intention consisting of a few paragraphs, outlining her feelings of regret and hope as she stands at the threshold of a new life in recovery. She can also choose a *tzedaka* project that would enable her to give something back.

In the rare circumstance that this ceremony be public, all the above could be included, plus an *aliya* blessing to the Torah on a Shabbat morning to symbolize her re-engagement in congregational life. Immediately after the *aliya* blessing she could recite the *Gomel* blessing. This prayer is recited by one who has emerged from a serious illness or life-threatening situation. Addiction would certainly be included in this category. The prayer reads: "Praised are You, Adonai our God, who rules the universe, showing goodness to us beyond our merits, for bestowing favor upon me." The congregation then responds in unison, "May God who has been gracious to you continue to favor you with all that is good." Just imagine the emotional power of this moment, when an individual returns to her community after the dark night of active addiction and treatment and is able to declare her gratitude and hope, followed by a resounding affirmation by the congregation. I understand that most individuals in early recovery might shy away from this type of public event and I cannot blame them. But for those who think otherwise, a brief synagogue ceremony could be immensely cathartic and inspiring.

Most Jews are secular in orientation and would not be inclined to immediately connect with a rabbi or synagogue after completing treatment. Though religion may not offer them a ready avenue for marking their return to home and community there are other ways to accomplish the same goal. Examples include 12 Step fellowships' awarding of coins or key chains following X days of sobriety, volunteering for a community organization, planting a garden, taking up a new creative endeavor. One could be free to develop any ritual or ceremony that would be meaningful. The intent is to recognize, either formally or informally, the transition from trauma to treatment to recovery instead of pretending that the re-entry should come easily and naturally.

One can only imagine the intensity of the leper's sense of isolation and loneliness while living in quarantine. Once the healing was confirmed by the priest and the quarantine lifted, the recovering leper would need to reckon with a myriad of mixed feelings. The same would hold true for anyone emerging from major sickness. This is aptly described in the commentary of "Etz Hayim," Conservative Judaism's version of the Torah with commentary: "The formal description of the cleansing ritual masks the deep and possibly conflicted feelings of the person who has recovered from a serious illness. These might include feelings of relief and happiness together with a new appreciation of good health, perhaps resentment over what had been gone through well as envy of people who had remained healthy. The offering of the leper is sometimes referred to as 'the sacrifice of one who has returned from the dead,' either because the illness was so grave or because a life cut off from all human contact, a life without friends and family, was not really a life."[2] Every word of this quote applies exactly to the condition of the addicted person who manages to find recovery!

The purification rituals included elements such as hyssop and a crimson thread, considered by the great commentator Rashi to be symbols of humility. Other commentators related the shaving of the head, another part of the purification rite, to the elimination of haughtiness. The recovering person is contending with such a range of feelings: fear, anxiety, disorientation, relief, joy, hope. He would do well to focus on humility, acknowledging that he didn't get there all on his own, that he benefited from the support of treatment professionals as well as family and friends. With the humility comes a profound sense of gratitude and the need to give back. The next task is to discover how best to accomplish this.

---

2   David Lieber, senior ed., *Etz Hayim: Torah and Commentary* (Philadelphia: Jewish Publication Society, 2001), p. 660.

Chapter 3

Paying it Forward

The last chapter focused primarily on the aftermath of inpatient rehab. However, the phenomenon of return after exile can also apply to completion of an outpatient treatment episode or even to the achievement of recovery without treatment. The fog of addiction is in itself a type of exile, a time of alienation from self and community as described in Part One of this volume. Once the individual emerges from this state, he will face new challenges regardless of whether he received treatment or whether he needed to be separated from family and community. The challenges may be more acute after an inpatient episode, partly due to the level of disorientation. For this reason, more experts are now advocating the option of outpatient treatment. The patient continues to live at home or elsewhere in the community while attending a regular or intensive outpatient program. If he had somehow managed to stay employed, he can still keep his job, receive a paycheck and figure out how to spend and save it responsibly. He can begin to improve key relationships while learning to sever the previous connections that kept him mired in drug use. Not everyone needs to go away in order to accomplish this. Inpatient rehab or no, the healing brain, body and spirit now face the realization that their old best friend, the drug of choice, can no longer be of service.

Much has been written about the addictive personality. One of the best books I have seen on the subject is Rabbi Abraham Twerski's *Addictive Thinking*.[1] The inclination to deceive oneself, to slip into irrational thought patterns in order to justify self-destructive behaviors is not exclusive to people with chemical dependence. I believe we all do this. I recall my clinical supervisor, Peggy Whelan, once telling me that whenever a patient asked her if she herself was in recovery she'd answer "we're all in recovery from some addiction." Yet the newly recovering individual is especially susceptible to a well-known pitfall: replacing one addiction with another.

---

1   Abraham Twerski, *Addictive Thinking: Understanding Self-Deception.* 2nd ed. (Minnesota: Hazelden, 1997).

Part Three – Recovery and Return

During my time in the clinic, it was not uncommon to see patients achieve abstinence or reduction of use from one drug only to develop a dependence on another. I interviewed several patients who stopped using illicit opioids with the aid of methadone or buprenorphine but started using alcohol, benzodiazepines, cocaine or marijuana. Our clinic continued to treat them because of our Harm Reduction philosophy and the recognition that they were getting help with accomplishing their Treatment Plan goal of stopping illicit opioid use. But we were still concerned that their new addiction could become equally if not more problematic. For this reason, one of our tasks as counselors was to help our patients understand the underlying emotional and thought patterns that made them tick. The need to self-medicate was the most common, often related to maladaptive coping behaviors generated by a trauma history. Trauma-based treatment is often essential when providing help for people with addiction disorders. Ignoring patients' trauma histories is like dressing a wound with Vaseline. The trauma is itself can often be part of the root cause of the addiction.

So our patients weren't necessarily out of the woods once they stopped using their drug of choice. We and they had to be on guard against the emergence of new harmful behaviors.

Drugs and alcohol weren't the only culprit. We saw cases of pathological gambling, eating disorders, sex addiction and compulsive video gaming. Though few of us had expertise in these areas, we found ourselves called upon to utilize the same therapeutic techniques to help the patients break the cycle. I don't know how effective we were in this regard. But I believe the treatment models that have been proven effective for some addictions can be successfully employed for other types of addiction.

What does this have to do with those who have completed treatment and who are in early remission from their condition? Even the best treatment will not necessarily root out addictive thinking or the need to find an outlet in different types of compulsive behaviors. People cannot be expected to be superhuman, neither the treatment providers or their patients. Once the treatment episode has ended, the recovering person's mind can still hover around darker places and the vulnerability doesn't miraculously disappear. The world presents triggers and temptations at every corner.

A gas station near my home has the following products featured on its road sign: coffee, cigarettes, ATM, lotto. Three out of four involve addictive activities, the fourth provides the outlet for funding the other three. There is no avoiding it. Addictive triggers are everywhere.

One of my patients in recovery from alcohol bragged about being able to walk into a package store to buy lotto tickets without purchasing liquor. I asked him two questions: 1. Why didn't he go to a convenience store or gas station to buy the lotto tickets instead? 2. How much money does he spend on this type of gambling? He didn't appreciate the line of questioning, but it got him to think about risky behaviors outside of alcohol consumption.

The period of early remission that coincides with the Action Stage of Change calls for extra vigilance. The person in recovery has already identified triggers and learned relapse prevention skills while in treatment. Now that he is adjusting to life in recovery, new triggers and urges may arise. The coping skills he learned in treatment are now put into action and can be applied to all sorts of addictive thinking and compulsions. But the vulnerability remains.

In Deuteronomy chapter 11, during Moses' series of final exhortations to the Israelites, he tells his people, "If you obey the commandments that I enjoin upon you this day...I will grant the rain for your land in season...I will also provide grass in the fields for your cattle – and thus you shall eat your fill. Take care not to be lured away to serve other gods and bow to them (Deuteronomy 11:13-16)." He was worried that, upon settling in the land of Canaan, the Israelites would become comfortable and sated and thus more susceptible to pagan influences. His worries were proven to be well founded. Despite the Book of Joshua's claim that the conquest of Canaan involved the obliteration of the seven Canaanite nations, we know from the Book of Judges that this didn't really happen. The Canaanite nations remained, and the pagan and idolatrous influences were ever present. The Book of Judges follows a repeated pattern of the peoples' sinning through idolatry followed their subjugation to a pagan nation, their cry for help, God's selection of a judge/deliverer, military victory against the pagan oppressors and eventual relapse into idolatry. Whenever things got good, the people turned away from their covenant with God.

The individual in recovery is equally susceptible. That makes his recovery strategy so important. At times he will want to tweak it or even abandon it and he will need to muster all the inner strength and outside support he can. Restoring family relationships, participating in a 12 Step fellowship (if that's for him), finding or regaining employment will serve as a strong line of defense against slips, relapse or developing another addiction. So will a return to hobbies, creative outlets and sports activities that attracted his interest before falling into addiction. I always found it useful to encourage my patients to consider resuming some pursuits that occupied them when they were young. The fact that they chose those particular activities indicates a proclivity and level of interest that is connected to their true personality, not the personality that would become addled by addiction. The patients were usually animated and excited when talking about this. They seemed motivated to pick up some of the healthy pursuits that they had onetime enjoyed.

I also highly recommend activities like worship, meditation, learning and exercise. Joining a faith community can be immensely rewarding. For many years, I have made it a practice to pray daily but sometimes I would do so in the solitude of my home. Over the past several years I have included daily attendance at a minyan (prayer quorum of 10) as part of my routine. Participating in a minyan does wonders for my state of mind. So does meditation. I meditate for 15 minutes every morning before going out to services. This sets a tone of serenity and equilibrium for my day. After breakfast, I take some time to study Jewish texts. Finally, I make sure to exercise daily. As these pursuits stimulate the endorphins, I feel more empowered to make the most out of each day. The same holds true for anyone in early or more advanced recovery. But the phase of early recovery is when self care is most called for.

Early in my rabbinic career I attended a workshop with the late psychologist Sol Gordon. This was during my years at my first pulpit in Columbus, Georgia. I may have been the only Jewish person in the auditorium that day. And here was Dr. Gordon, going on at length about a concept he coined "Mitzvah Therapy." He suggested that the performance of *mitzvot*, especially those involving helping other people (*Gemilut Hasadim*), serves a therapeutic value. When we are feeling depressed and anxious, doing something for someone else helps lift us out of our melancholy and supplies us with a sense of self-worth and value. The satisfaction we gain by helping others is detectable in brain activity; the performance of *mitzvot* sends a message to the amygdala, the emotional center of the brain. The result: We get cheered up when we do for others.

The recovering person will experience emotional highs and lows as she proceeds through the recovery journey. She may feel that she's doing all the right things, or at least doing her best, when a setback occurs. Self-doubt and vulnerability creep in. That is precisely the time when mitzvah therapy can be most effective. It also works as a type of prophylactic measure to store up positive emotions and self-worth when times are good.

Paying it forward is a way of combining mitzvah therapy with showing gratitude. The recovering person becomes more aware of all the kindnesses done for her in the past. She may not have the chance to repay the benefactors directly, so she seeks out ways to perform similar kindnesses to others. In so doing, she adds an extra dimension of power and personal growth to her recovery. She can do this on an individual level or through volunteer work. Either way, she is achieving the same end: to lift herself out of her self and into the realm of service. Her former life in addiction was the ultimate destructive type of self service. Now in recovery, she is able to harness her impulse to do good on behalf of others. Though she is not primarily motivated by personal gain, the emotional and spiritual rewards will be great.

As the months tick by, the Action Stage of Change will move into the Maintenance Stage. A new life pattern in recovery has taken hold. Yet the ground can remain shaky, not only for the recovering individual but for family members as well. Memories of erratic, disturbing behaviors from the addiction period linger. If trauma was involved, the aftereffects can persist and require attention, possibly on a therapy level. Trust is not re-established immediately. The memories of several years of disturbing behaviors can hardly be expected to fade within weeks or a few months. So the family usually stays on a heightened state of vigilance. This is sometimes necessary. But it can backfire.

Healthy detachment and perspective are key. Family members need to give the recovering person the space to find her way, make her own mistakes and learn from them. Old habits of rushing in to rescue, enable and interfere ought to be overcome at this stage. Otherwise, growth in recovery may be interrupted and additional tensions may arise.

To the family members: If and when you notice or suspect troubling behaviors, be extra careful. Before you say anything, use the old Al-Anon acronym **THINK** – standing for: Is it **T**houghtful, **H**onest, **I**ntelligent, **N**ecessary and **K**ind? If one of these considerations is absent, hold your tongue. You will soon know whether to say anything and how to say it. Otherwise, your well-meaning but unsolicited comment could backfire. Al-Anon, Nar-Anon and good self-help books about healthy detachment can provide you with some guidelines.

To the recovering individual: Cut your family members and friends some slack. They are not used to you as you are now. They have to get to know you all over again. The person they once knew became overshadowed and distorted by the addiction; now that old person is re-emerging, but you are not the same as you once were. So if they say something mistrustful, if they convey suspicion, try to let it pass. Don't let it derail you. Everyone is learning to rebuild the relationships, and the learning curve can be steep. Be patient.

Chapter 4

PAWS

The Fifth Stage of Change, the Maintenance Stage, typically begins about six months after the beginning of recovery. In this phase, the recovering individual intends to maintain healthy behaviors and avoid the pitfalls of relapse. The Maintenance Stage usually calls for a high level of determination and a concerted effort to practice the tools of relapse prevention and positive coping skills. The person in recovery has achieved success in avoiding temptation, but thoughts of relapse can still occur, and the triggers are everywhere.

For the effected individuals and families, Post Acute Withdrawal Syndrome (PAWS) is a phenomenon that must be taken seriously. According to the website Addictions and Recovery (www.addictionsandrecovery.org), PAWS is a condition marked by a reduction in physical symptoms and an increase in emotional and psychological withdrawal symptoms. The formerly addicted brain is gradually healing. The brain chemistry is in flux. PAWS symptoms can include mood swings, increased irritability and anxiety, fatigue, lulls in enthusiasm, the tendency to take on too much, variable concentration and disturbed sleep. All these symptoms are really positive signs that the brain and psyche are getting better.[1]

One fact that can be especially discouraging: PAWS can last months, even years. Two years is not uncommon. Yet this can also be comforting. When the recovering individual is still feeling anxious and overwhelmed after a year or more, she can reassure herself by knowing she is going through a condition that is normal, predictable and well-documented.

Here's a typical scenario: Phil has been in recovery over a year and is feeling well. He has made excellent progress. He is hopeful. The pink cloud is still hanging over him to some extent and he convinces himself that he can take on several new responsibilities to make up

---

1   Information about PAWS found online at https://www.addictionsandrecovery.org/post-acute-withdrawal.htm and at the SAMHSA website https://store.samhsa.gov/system/files/sma10-4554.pdf

for the time lost while in the throes of addiction. Phil has found full time employment and is performing reasonably well in the workplace. Meanwhile, he decides to enroll part time in a college program with the hope of eventually getting a degree. He is also working to rebuild relationships that had been damaged in the past. He goes to AA meetings, has a sponsor and has also started to take on sponsees himself.

A few weeks into the college semester he starts to notice that he is feeling frustrated and discouraged. He's having trouble concentrating on his studies. He's not functioning as well at work. He's getting increasingly irritable at home. He's losing patience with the people around him, and the relationships he has been rebuilding are getting frayed. Phil winds up dropping out of school and decides to renew focus on his job and his home life. For a while, he considers himself a failure until his therapist reminds him that he is still in post acute withdrawal. He is experiencing the normal, predictable symptoms of someone in this phase of recovery. The symptoms were aggravated when he took on the extra task of going back to school. He really wasn't ready for it. He hadn't given his brain and psyche enough time to heal before taking on new and challenging responsibilities.

PAWS can be challenging not only to the individual but to the affected family members. They have undergone so much stress and tension for so long. Now that their loved one is in recovery and several months have passed, they expect a return to full normalcy (whatever that is! – I've heard it said that the only "normal" is a setting on a washing machine). Instead, they notice symptoms that make them wonder whether the recovery is really genuine. They might catch themselves thinking: "I thought she was doing so much better. What's happened? Is she relapsing?" They are unaware that post acute withdrawal is happening and it is actually part of the long-term healing process.

The key word here is patience; patience for the recovering person and patience for her family and friends. Months, even years transpire and the healing goes on. For the family, the healing involves rebuilding trust, continuing to work on themselves, developing a healthy physical, emotional and spiritual life style. For the recovering person, the healing calls for an ongoing dedication to the individualized recovery plan that has helped her all along.

Patience is far from automatic. It comes through self help and God's help. In my view, it is one of the hardest qualities to achieve.

I know because I still struggle with it, after so many years and so much personal work. Prayer, meditation, exercise all play a vital role. Attitude is essential. The 7th Step in the 12 Step philosophy can be helpful here: "Humbly asked Him to remove all our shortcomings." After undergoing a thorough moral and spiritual inventory and becoming ready to move beyond our shortcomings, we take the leap by asking God to remove them. We recognize that these shortcomings are no longer of use to us. Perhaps they served us well in the past, perhaps we needed to hold on to them. But now we are ready to change specific attitudes and behaviors because we realize how much harm they can cause. For me, as well as for so many others, impatience is an attitude that becomes highly toxic. Once we understand this, we can turn to God in humility, through supplication, prayer and meditation, ask God to help us develop more patience; patience with ourselves and with others. As the recovery journey progresses into the long term, this is a lesson that applies equally to the recovering individual as well as his loved ones.

PAWS is actually a blessing in disguise. Imagine you sustain an injury while exercising. Your doctor and physical therapist provide you with a specific, detained regimen for healing. You follow their recommendations and, in time, notice you are getting better. But every so often you move a certain way or momentarily forget about the injury during an instant of recklessness, and a shot of pain suddenly reminds you that you are not completely healed. That little wake-up call helps you regain focus on the recovery plan that heretofore has served you so well.

In the same way, the symptoms of PAWS are the alarm signaling the recovering individual (and his loved ones) to regain focus and concentration on the plan that has helped him (and them) achieve such impressive progress; for him, progress in recovery, sobriety and the ability to lead a productive life; for them, progress in healthy, loving detachment, and self-care. So when the symptoms pop up, when he is feeling overwhelmed, irritable, somehow off kilter, he (and they) would do well to remember that he is experiencing something that is perfectly normal, a syndrome that is both common and predictable, one that will eventually fade and disappear.

In addition to impatience, one nasty nemesis lurks for those anticipating a long-term stable recovery or even a cure: complacency. Both attitudes can easily spur a relapse.

There may be some people who actually find themselves cured

of their addiction disease. This is the exception rather than the rule. These fortunate individuals are able to eventually move beyond their recovery plan and stop worrying about relapse prevention and coping skills to prevent relapse. They consider themselves to be safe. Perhaps they are. But such people are exceedingly rare.

The vast majority of recovering individuals need to engage in a long-term, even lifelong battle with the insidious shadow of their previous addiction. If they become complacent or let down their guard, trouble can ensue. As the months and years in recovery go by, the safety level will probably increase. But for most people, the danger never completely disappears.

If a person achieves recovery through treatment or through self help programs like AA or NA, she learns a series of recovery tools that help her navigate the rocky path of healing from addiction. She fills her toolbox, as it were, with strategies and skills that she invariably picks up from others who have used them successfully. The tools typically include the people/places/things that were described in Part Two, chapter 9. Attending meetings, communal worship, avoiding risky environments and situations, staying away from former acquaintances with whom one used drugs, focusing on a healthy lifestyle, utilizing positive coping skills and the power of positive thinking, maintaining good boundaries, all these are examples of effective tools that support people in short and long-term recovery. Once these tools get put aside, the threat of relapse creeps back in.

When a person suffers from clinical depression and is fortunate enough to find a helpful professional and an effective medication, he begins to experience a return to normalcy and the promise of a happier life. At a certain point, he may say to himself, "I'm feeling like myself again, I'm not depressed any longer, I don't really need this medicine anymore." He forgets that the medication has been an integral part of his successful recovery plan and convinces himself that he can stave off the depression on his own. Then the inevitable happens. Without the medication, and without the support of a dedicated professional, he begins to spiral back into depression. Cases like this happen all the time.

Similarly with addiction, when the toolbox gets put aside, relapse can overtake one before he can even muster the ability to gather up and use those tools again. Before he knows it, he sees himself back to square one. All because he decided to neglect the very strategies and tactics that brought him into a successful recovery in the first place.

Consider the following: Jim struggled for years with alcohol dependence until he found his way to treatment and AA. He achieved sobriety. Jim started attending AA meetings almost daily, took on service positions, got himself a sponsor and eventually became a sponsor himself. He lived and breathed the program. As the years went on, Jim slowly began to lighten his commitment to AA. He started attending 3 or 4 meetings a week, cut down on his service responsibilities. Instead of calling his sponsor every day like he had done earlier, he began calling every other day. He reasoned that he was feeling stable in his sobriety while his work, family and social activities were making it harder to keep up his AA commitment level. Jim told himself that he was experiencing no cravings for alcohol, that he had managed to fill up his life with enough healthy activities and was too busy to even think about returning to the bottle.

After about seven years in recovery Jim wound up attending meetings only once or twice a week, turned down all service opportunities and even gave up his sponsees, informing them he was too busy to give them the time and attention they needed. This pattern continued for close to two years. Then, almost without warning, Jim relapsed. He found himself at a party after an especially difficult week at work. Without asking if it was OK, someone put a glass of scotch in his hand. For a fleeting moment Jim thought about handing it back. Then he took a swig. He suddenly felt as if all the problems of the workweek had disappeared and the scotch tasted and felt so good, so he drank some more. Before he knew it, Jim was back into alcoholism.

The complacency that crept into Jim's attitudes about recovery is what doomed him. As he gradually removed the tools of his recovery from daily life, he became more susceptible to the inevitable relapse. The recovery plan that had worked so well had, ironically, allowed him to feel as if he didn't need it anymore. The results were sadly predictable.

The recovery plan need not be determined by a 12 Step program. It can be anything safe and reasonable that works for the individual. Whatever the plan is, if it works for a while and is eventually put aside out of complacency and over-confidence, the risks for relapse increase accordingly.

The symptoms of PAWS are a wake-up call during the Maintenance Stage of Change: This is not the time to grow smug or over-relaxed in recovery. Recovery takes immense work, even once the remission from the drug has become sustained and long term. In fact, one may claim that in some ways the work becomes harder, because the impulse to lay off and put the tools aside can be quite seductive. The more comfortable in recovery one becomes, the more vulnerable one truly is.

In Biblical terms, idolatry is the inclination to turn away from God as the source of truth, light and healing and towards idols or gods that bring only falsehood and conceit. During Moses' last days, this was precisely his concern about the Israelites' future. In Deuteronomy, Moses delivers his final lectures and prophecies to the people. He warns them that after they settle in Canaan, they and their descendants will become complacent and spiritually indolent: "So Jeshurun grew fat and kicked – You grew fat and gross and coarse – He forsook the God who made him and spurned the Rock of his support... You neglected the Rock that begot you. Forgot the God who brought you forth. (Deuteronomy 32:15,18)"[2] The prophet is predicting that following the conquest of Canaan, the people will become satiated with their physical needs and will begin to forget the One who made it all possible. They will grow too comfortable in their own land and in their newly found state of freedom. They will turn to Canaanite gods and abandon their own unique recovery tool kit – the Covenant, embodied in the Torah and its *mitzvot*.

So Moses decides to impart a poem of warning, found in the Torah portion *Ha'azinu* (Deuteronomy 32) to the people with the purpose of having them memorize it and transmit it to future generations. The poem is a prophecy that contrasts the Israelites' faithlessness with God's reliability. They are described as treacherous, disloyal and neglectful. They turn their backs on the Covenant. As a result, God will punish them. But God will never abandon them and will ultimately vindicate and redeem them. The poem is meant to be a witness for future generations, a kind of "I told you so!" whenever the people complain of the consequences of their idolatry. And it is meant to be a warning to anyone willing to heed its message by rejecting idolatry and embracing the Covenant.

Life in addiction is a kind of idolatry. It robs a person of her spiritual core. It creates a chasm between the addicted person and her Creator. It sets up a straw man of meaninglessness and vanity. Like the Israelites who suffered under Egyptian slavery and eventually would find a purposeful way by accepting the Torah at Sinai and the

---

2   Biblical Hebrew grammar often places future verbs in the past tense – Moses is really prophesying the future here.

promise of a free national existence after the Canaanite conquest, the recovering individual has emerged from the enslavement of addiction into a new life in recovery. Yet she can never totally let down her guard. She must accept the reality of her ongoing struggle and resist complacency. Even as her recovery advances into the long term, she must know that the idols of self-satisfaction and smugness threaten to ultimately separate her from her Higher Power; she may eventually give up her recovery plan, her own covenant with the healing power that has gotten her to where she is. And in turning her back on her recovery covenant, her tool box, she opens herself to the harmful forces that brought her into addiction in the first place.

Long-term recovery is a blessing to both the addicted person and her loved ones. It can bring serenity, hope and renewed life. It also demands constant vigilance for all concerned. If they practice self-care and stick to whatever plans had worked for them all along, they face a future filled with the promise of emotional and spiritual health.

Friends and loved ones will join together with a caring community to provide a sympathetic and supportive environment to all those in recovery. Synagogues will be proud to welcome their participation, whether or not they choose to disclose their history. They will take on leadership roles in the Jewish community. The entire community will recognize the recovering individual's great potential for making a significant contribution to Jewish life. For it is the rare person who can claim the level of tenacity, will, faith and dedication that the recovering individual has shown. In this light, she becomes a blessing not only to herself and her loved ones, but to the entire Jewish people.

Epilogue

We will not stop addiction by cajoling, censuring, stigmatizing or withholding vital evidence-based treatment. We will not help people by pretending that Judaism and Torah have all the answers. Only when we learn empathy towards those who suffer from the condition, only when we stop ostracizing and avoiding them and learn to honor and respect them by seeing them as children of God – only then will a caring and loving community find ways to support addicted individuals and their families as they seek the light of recovery.

A Hasidic story:
A revered rabbi became dangerously ill and the inhabitants of his town proclaimed a fast and communal prayer for his recovery. A member of a nearby village entered the town and went to the tavern to drink brandy. Several townsfolk overheard him ordering the drink and informed him that drinking was forbidden for the day, while the community was praying for the rabbi.

The visitor immediately went to the nearest synagogue and prayed: "O Lord, please cure the holy rabbi, so that I may have my drink."

Soon afterward the rabbi began to recover his strength and said, "The prayer of the visitor was more acceptable than any of yours. His prayer expressed the greatest longing and the most earnest supplication for my speedy recovery!"[1]

Addiction is powerful and all-consuming. The accompanying cravings are real. They can do great harm to the individual and her loved ones. Yet the rabbi in this story, instead of judging and condemning the visitor, chooses to laud him and express appreciation for the sincerity of his prayer, a prayer that was motivated by the compulsion to feed his addiction. Would that we, as a Jewish community, could hold such an attitude. Then, perhaps, we might see things change for the better.

Ben Azzai used to say: Do not scorn anyone at all and do not disparage (even inanimate) things – for there are no individuals who

---

1   Paraphrased from Louis I. Newman, *A Hasidic Anthology*, (New York: Shocken Books, 1963), p. 64.

do not have their day, nor any things that do not have their place (Pirkei Avot 4:3).⁽²⁾

The disease of addiction, which brings such scorn and derision in its wake, can cause us to ignore the goodness and spiritual worth of those who are afflicted. Yet as Ben Azzai reminds us, we all have our day, when our value is recognized by ourselves and others. Those "blessed" with addiction, will have their day too. Through human kindness, wisdom and God's help, healing and recovery will ultimately prevail.

יַעַנְךָ יי בְּיוֹם צָרָה יְשַׂגֶּבְךָ שֵׁם אֱלֹהֵי יַעֲקֹב:

The Lord will answer you in times of trouble,
the name of the God of Jacob will protect you.
(Psalm 20:1)

---

2   Translated by Martin S. Cohen, *Pirkei Avot Lev Shalem: The Wisdom of Our Sages* (New York, The Rabbinical Assembly, 2018), p. 176.

CPSIA information can be obtained
at www.ICGtesting.com
Printed in the USA
FSHW021218020719